MEMORIES OF COTTINGHAM STATION

DAVID KAY

DAVID KAY

Copyright © 2019 David Kay

First published in Great Britain in 2019 by Riverhead

All rights reserved.
No part of this publication may be reproduced,
stored in a retrieval system, or transmitted, in any form or
by any means, without the prior written permission of the
publisher, nor be otherwise circulated in any form of
binding or cover other than that in which it is published
and without a similar condition being imposed on the
subsequent publisher.

David Kay has asserted his right to be identified
as the author of this work under the Copyright, Designs
and Patents Act 1988.

A CIP catalogue record for this book is
available from the British Library

ISBN 978-1-9164294-4-4

Design and Production by Riverhead
Kardomah 94,
94 Alfred Gelder Street, Hull HU1 2AN
Telephone: 07890 170063
email: mike.riverheadbooks@gmail.com

Printed by: Fisk Printers, Hull

MEMORIES OF COTTINGHAM STATION

ACKNOWLEDGEMENTS

The following publications have greatly assisted in the writing of
"Memories of Cottingham Station":
Kingston Upon Hull AZ Street Atlas
British Railways North Eastern Region Passenger Services Timetable, 1963/64 Winter Edition
Pullman by Julian Morel
Pullman Trains in Britain by R.W.Kidner - Oakwood Press
Ian Allan British Railways Locomotives and other motive power, several editions from 1956/7, 1961 & 1968
BR Steam Motive Power Depots, North Eastern Region by Paul Bolger
British Railways Locomotives Cut Up by Drapers of Hull by Brian Egan and Ian Scotney - Hutton Press Ltd of 1989.
Lost Railways of North & East Yorkshire by Gordon Suggitt
(with help on Butlin's Filey Holiday Camp branch)
Cottingham Then & Now by Rachel Waters
Hull Daily Mail for information on Cottingham North signalbox's withdrawal
Marsden Rail dvd No.12 - HULL
and thanks to *Google* on two occasions for their help.
And finally, I would like to give my grateful and never ending thanks to my sister Susan for giving me the inspiration to start writing. She's on Facebook and always sending me old photographs of Cottingham Station, some ancient, some not so old and from 'my day' as a trainspotter. When one arrived with a very long annotation about its history, that was it.
That gave me the idea. Thanks a million, Sue.

DAVID KAY

FRONT COVER PHOTOGRAPHS:
Top: No.92220 "Evening Star" heads north with the "Scarborough Spa Express"
Bottom: A Gresley A4 streamliner, No.19 "Bittern" heads north through Cottingham with a Charter Special.

BACK COVER PHOTOGRAPH:
The late artist & wildlife conservationist, David Shepherd's 9F freight engine 92203 "Black Prince" on the North Norfolk Railway. We saw a few of these engines, grimy and very work stained on our 25/- runabout tickets in 1966 & 67. Only "Evening Star", the last one, was named and painted in Swindon green in 1960.

PHOTOGRAPHS:
Whilst every effort has been made to contact the relevant copyright holders, unless otherwise stated, all the images used in this book are either the property of the author or were sourced from the internet.

MEMORIES OF COTTINGHAM STATION

FOREWORD

Thankyou for picking up "MEMORIES OF COTTINGHAM STATION". I take it you are or have been sometime in the past, a commuter or shopper, getting your train from those platforms of Cottingham to Hull, Beverley or perhaps much further afield?

Or even a dedicated life-long enthusiast like myself? Today Cottingham Station is completely lifeless and without character and with all the windows and doors boarded up and out of use and probably rotting away inside, too. Do you remember the wooden northern extension on the Hull-bound platform? Perhaps not. Do you remember home starter signals, particularly one on the Hull side right at the end of the platform slope with it's very tall post? There may even have been a water column there at one time, but its hardly a wisp in my memory. This was for topping up tanks for the last four miles into Hull during the steam train era of the 1950s. Do you remember the four or more staff busying themselves with various duties including the collection of everybody's tickets at the two wicket gates? Do you remember the winter fires burning in the Hull side waiting room? Do you remember the morning shunt in the goods yard with a large, ex-War Department freight engine from 50B Hull Dairycoates shed? Do you remember the Cattle Dock? The signal boxes at Thwaite Gates & Cottingham North road crossings? Do you remember the steam-hauled summer special excursion trains belting through the platforms on a Saturday and

Uncle Ron & I at Hornsea Town, 1955

Sunday, morning and evening?

Well I do remember all this and more, as I take you on a full tour in 'Memories Of Cottingham Station' with an excursion of my own to Waterworks crossing by Ideal Standard Radiator and Boiler Works and then to the bufferstops of platforms 1 to 14 of Hull Paragon, my Mecca, where I would see the most majestic train of all: The five-coach portion of Hull's very own "Yorkshire Pullman" taking the rich and famous on the first part of their journeys to London and perhaps even to Europe! This was the 1960s and I was growing up fast. My Great Aunt introduced me to the fabulous world of trains and railways and here I am, now a pensioner and still working and still extremely passionate about railways, particularly in Britain. "Railways in my Blood" would have been an alternative title about my passion for Cottingham Station where I grew up. I do hope you enjoy my book. I've thoroughly enjoyed writing every word with that passion. Happy reading.

MEMORIES OF COTTINGHAM STATION

INTRODUCTION

As you can see in the accompanying photograph, this was my very first sighting of a train. It's Hornsea Town Station in 1955 and there's me with my Uncle Ron, Dad's only living brother, as the younger one, who would have been my Uncle David, was killed during WW2 at the tender age of just twenty-one. I've visited David's grave in the Netherlands on two occasions. I'm named after him and very proud too!

Here I am then, just two years old. Strangely enough, I never went to Hornsea by train. Uncle Ron always had a car as did another distant relative we called Auntie Joan. Even the sister branch to Withernsea, we only went once by train as described later in the book. The engine we can see here is probably a Raven A8 tank, but more about these in the first chapter.

This book is about my life from the 1950s as a small child to leaving school in 1970, when I finally decided it was time to scrap my notebook, pen and classic ABC Ian Allan pocket books. Its a list of anecdotes about visiting Cottingham Station throughout these years, with spotting from a footbridge on the way to Hull Paragon Station - my Mecca for trains, thrown in for good measure. I still love this classic trainshed, but Hull is also now but a former shadow of its former glory of the heyday of railways and steam traction. I've loved every second of writing "Memories Of Cottingham Station", I hope you enjoy the read. It will be my only production, so please don't look for sequels. You can only write about what you are passionate of and my childhood is just that...and always will be. Read on....

You will need to know of some abbreviations I use profusely throughout the book:-
BG   Gangwayed Brake van with no passenger accomodation but still looking like a passenger carriage but with fewer and smaller windows.
bhp   Brake horse power.
BR   British Railways, 1948-1997 when it was fully privatised. This was shortened to British Rail in the 1965 Modernisation Plan, when the white, double-arrow logo was introduced and still identifies stations, even today.
CAD   Computer aided design in helping to gather data for new-build steam locomotive projects.
'copped'   You won't find this word in the Oxford dictionary! Its purely trainspotters slang for seeing a number for the first time. This is when it got underlined in our Ian Allan ABC pocket books.
DfT   Department for Transport.
DMU   is a diesel multiple unit, first introduced in 1954 and would become the train of the present and future and what I grew up with.
DVT   Driving van trailer on the opposite end to an electric hauled train.
ECML   London to Edinburgh main line including Leeds, Hull, Skipton & Sunderland.
EYMS   East Yorkshire Motor Services. In 2018, bought out by a North Eastern concern *Go-Ahead* and the company name shortened to just 'East Yorkshire'.
GNER   Great North Eastern Railway franchise ran briefly: 1996-2006.
HST125 High speed train unit capable of 125 miles per hour and now over forty years old and still going strong in

MEMORIES OF COTTINGHAM STATION

Scotland and The West Country but with shorter formations.
LMS London Midland & Scottish Railway, in existence from 1923-1947.
LNER London and North Eastern Railway, in existence from 1923-1947. And used again from 2018 as a franchisee on the **ECML,** but as a completely new company.
MPD Motive power depot or engine shed where locomotives are stabled overnight and serviced.
NRM National Railway Museum, Leeman Road, York - the best in the world!
ORR The Government Office for Rail and Road (formerly Office of Rail Regulation).
RHTT Railhead treatment train sprays the track during the leaf fall season.
SO/SX Saturdays Only and Saturdays Excepted as shown in timetables.
TOC Train Operating Company is either a franchise or Open Access company.
TOPS In 1973, British Rail introduced a new computerised network system, short for '**Total Operations Processing System**'. So as an example, D6732 and now a resident of the North Norfolk Railway in East Anglia, originally based at Hull 50B shed, would be renumbered 37 032 and later 37 353, replicating continental practice.
VTEC Virgin Trains East Coast operating along **ECML** routes including Hull.
WD War Department Austerity 2-8-0 goods engines acting as shunters or station pilots in the text, but built for heavy-haul freight work.

Today we take the 24 Hour clock for granted. It wasn't until 1964 that British Railways and London Transport introduced this modern way of telling the time. I have an old timetable dated 9th September 1963 to 14th June 1964 used extensively in the preparation of this book and would be the very last such publication to use old timing descriptions of **'am' and 'pm'.** But I love it and it adds character to the text. You may obtain copies of these old railway timetables covering any of the six BR regions you like, at various online sites, from Robert Humm's second-hand transport bookshop in Stamford, Lincolnshire or by calling at the **Vintage Carriages Trust Museum of Rail Travel (The Rail Story) in Ingrow Yard on the Keighley and Worth Valley Railway in West Yorkshire.** We keep them in the magazine room where I volunteer. Just ask in the shop, please. We have Continental timetables too!

MEMORIES OF COTTINGHAM STATION

CONTENTS

Steam Train to Bridlington	13
Diesel Multiple Units	27
Cottingham Station's history	37
Its 1960 and I'm old enough	43
The Morning Shunt	87
The 25/- Weekly Runabout ticket	93
Steam bows out at Cottingham	111
Hull & Barnsley tracks	116
Hull Paragon, my Mecca of trains	119
Family excursions from Hull Paragon	141
The closed doors of British Rail	149
The Modern Scene	151
Footnote: The demise of trainspotting	159

DAVID KAY

A northbound train at Cottingham during the Edwardian period. Note the wooden platform extension on the left.

… MEMORIES OF COTTINGHAM STATION

CHAPTER 1
STEAM TRAIN TO BRIDLINGTON

I first stepped foot on the tarmac of Cottingham station platforms in 1956 when I was just three years old. I was being lifted over the footboards and into the compartment of a Gresley corridor third. 1956 was the last year of third class that had stayed on the railways for most of the 20th century. Third class finally became second class in that year and was consigned to the history books for ever. I was travelling with the Camp family (my mothers side) on an ill-fated holiday (for me), to Bridlington where we stayed in an apartment over the other side to *Seacrest Boarding House* in Sands Lane, where my parents would take me and Jonathan (my younger brother), some years later. A few days later, I was being rushed home by road as I was seriously ill with pneumonia. I believe my Grandfather's business partner, Alf Hirst did the honours. The confines of a train compartment was not the place for a very sick little boy. This was the only time in my life that I could easily have passed away!

At the age of three, I remember there being something big, dirty and black at the front of my first train journey. It could have been anything. One of Robinson's A5 tanks introduced in 1911 or Raven's similar class A8 of 1913, rebuilt by Sir Nigel Gresley in

Another classic undated view at Cottingham looking towards Thwaite Gates & Hull.

An original shedplate posing as a house number, off a steam locomotive smokebox door, allocated to 55A shed at Leeds Holbeck. You can bid for these plates at a railwayana auction, but expect to pay upwards of £100. Sighting them in antique shop windows would be rare!

MEMORIES OF COTTINGHAM STATION

LNER's new 'Azuma' unit, around 7am for the business traveller. Eight trains to London! My 1963/64 timetable shows just two such workings during that winter, one the prestigious *Yorkshire Pullman*, described in much detail in an earlier chapter. There may have been a third and fourth in the Summer only and I know one ran at 1645hrs later on, on a Sunday afternoon as I used it myself in 1973 when returning to London during a lengthy training course with Thomas Cooks at their then, Berkeley Street (off Piccadilly) headquarters.

Its 2019 and *Hull Trains* has really been struggling with reliability issues for the last few months now, due to technical faults and crash damage involving most of the four sets (none spare these days) and one set even had a fire on board at Grantham. I was checking the live departures app to find the next mornings departure time and it wasn't shown. The *Hull Trains* service from Beverley wasn't running. February 2019 and they have finally taken the sensible measure of hiring-in a cascaded five-car, HST125 set from sister company *First Great Western* to resolve their immediate dilemma. This was seen recently travelling through Doncaster and Thorne North, with the buffet car in Great Western's new stylish dark green livery, whereas all other coaches used the previous dark blue with futuristic 'dynamic lines'.

The first set of a five-train, £60 million order by Hull Trains for Hitachi class 802, AT300 bi-mode units, is due to arrive in the UK at the end of August 2019. The sets are being built at Pistoia in Italy, using bodyshells manufactured in Kasado, Japan. Railway Magazine for July 2019, tells me the first set is expected to be in service by the time this book appears in print. Notice that they've ordered one extra set to cope with maintenance and repairs, etc. A state of the art, 21st.century high-spec, 140mph capable train will actually call at Cottingham Station on the Beverley to London service, from November 2019. These five Class 802 units will be called "The Paragon fleet" to reflect the Northern terminus of their designated route from London Kings Cross at Hull.

The LNER's 0700 'Hull Executive' became the first such, revenue-earning service for that company on Wednesday 15th.May, being used for the remainder of the day on a Kings Cross/Leeds diagram before returning to Hull in the evening and then back to Doncaster, empty stock. A first for Hull!

I'm just waiting for the day that **DfT** (Department for Transport), **ORR** (Office of Rail & Road) and *Network Rail* raise the line speed on main lines to 140mph as many of todays trains are well capable of this speed and have been, since introduced nearly thirty years ago (IC225 mark 4 sets with DVT & Virgin West Coast Italian-built 'Pendolinos') and saving passengers even more time. The future looks fantastic...I cannot wait!

And Cottingham Station's future looks secure too. I'm happy to report, that the railways are expanding once more, including opening new lines and stations as well as updating moribund freight only lines, as the public are demanding more and more travel opportunities and a better train frequency to cope with demand as well as more facilities including device charging points and digital information screens on all station platforms and in carriages too.

MEMORIES OF COTTINGHAM STATION

And on the spotter/enthusiast front, train liveries and fleet colours are getting more and more varied just as they would have been pre-grouping, prior to 1923, nearly one hundred years ago. Have we gone full circle? The only down side is that most modern trains are formed of multiple units and seeing a loco at the front can now be a rarity. But us dedicated and lifelong train buffs are still interested in all around us, if it runs on tracks...trams included!

Just in the nick of time before publishing, I've discovered another journal of sixties trainspotting activities and not at a steam heritage railway either, but at the National Tramway Museum at Crich in Derbyshire: **Shed Bashing with The Beatles, a trainspotter in the swinging sixties by Phil Mathison. Dead Good Publications 2006.** To me, Phil must have been the UK's most prolific trainspotter of all time, as in the five years between 1963 & 1967 inclusive, he 'copped' every one of over 5400 steam locos still in operation by that date. Whats more amazing, even at twelve years old, his Mum allowed him to go gallivanting off all over the country on his own or with friends (Dad was at sea) and his aim was to 'bash' every steam shed on the network. All 157 of them, even getting the ferry over the Solent to cover the Isle of Wight, still steam dominated until the last day of 1966. Many sheds, he called at several times. All I can say is that Phil must have had an extremely trusting mother and deep pocket money reserves. His quest for underlining everything was achieved with just one year and three weeks to spare before steam finished altogether. As you've read earlier, we were thirteen

Top: Unit 158 910 at Hull Paragon. Ve[ry] rarely, will you find another unit coupled [to it] and only when business demands this 'dou[ble] heading', as us trainspotters called it.

Bottom: A modern view of Hull Paragon trainshed taken from Park Street bridge. Note that only the south side is now used. A two car class 158 DMU is leaving on a glorious evening.

MEMORIES OF COTTINGHAM STATION

1931. These large, powerful tank engines were Pacific locomotives with their 4-6-2 wheel arrangement and based at Hull sheds as described later.

The A5, A7 & A8's were allocated locally at the then 53A Hull Dairycoates and 53B Hull Botanic Gardens MPDs where the local engine allocations were serviced. There was also the former Hull & Barnsley shed at Springhead, coded 53C, with Hull Alexandra Dock as its sub-shed. There was in 1956/57 even a steam shed at Bridlington coded 53D. I did cycle to Springhead Depot once on my travels, but by the mid-1960s it was just a rusting shell and derelict. One Hull-based A8 example carried the number 69858. The last few Raven A7 heavy tank locos also survived at 53A in 1956, but yet strangely enough no A6 engines ever existed. The local allocations where at 53B Hull Botanic Gardens depot before it was turned over to diesel operation in 1959/60 for the masses of DMUs that were to invade the Hull area. By the time I started spotting trains in 1960, all these Pacific tanks had long been transferred to 51D shed at Middlesbrough and some even scrapped. By 1961, they'd all gone to the scrapyard.

In case you're wondering, classes A1 to A4 were the East Coast 'racehorses' that frequented the main line, reaching speeds of 100 m.p.h. on a daily basis, although Edward Thompson's A2s were mainly seen north of the Border in Scotland.

There was a class of steam engine allocated to the Eastern and North Eastern Regions of British Railways that just eluded me. My 1961 ABC Ian Allan Combined Volume shows that eight of the Gresley D49 Hunt and Shire class, named after Counties of England and

DAVID KAY

Scotland and classic foxhunts of the area the locos served, were still extant by February of that year. I may even have seen one pass the platforms at Cottingham in 1960 or 61. I will never know, as I stupidly never kept my old ABC books! Something I now very much regret with great sadness. Half of these eight D49s had been named after Scottish Shires. They would have been lined out in LNER apple green in their glory days, but became unloved and neglected in their last days of service, so I just missed these fabulous 4-4-0 engines with their curved splasher nameplates. I really had been 'born too late'. They were scrapped later in 1961, but not by Albert Drapers in Hull as they hadn't started in the engine cutting business by then.

Later that year, just one D49/2 'Hunt' class remained. It was No.62747 "The Percy" (a foxhunt around Alnwick in Northumberland...pronounced Annick) and in 1950 had been allocated to 52C shed (MPD) at Blaydon, Newcastle. I can find no further reference to its allocation in 1959 in my North Eastern Region steam era shed book, so presume it must have been reallocated to a former London Midland shed in the West Riding. Most of the Scottish Shire locos were appropriately allocated to Scottish sheds and one, 62712 "Morayshire" is today normally found on the Bo'ness & Kinneil preserved railway in that country, in British Railways lined black livery.

1957 I believe, was my formal introduction to the wonderful world of railways. I had two great aunts, Alice & her sister Mary, both sisters of my grandfather Camp, my mother's father. It is Mary who we're concerned with. She was a spinster and rented a room in

MEMORIES OF COTTINGHAM STATION

a house in De Grey Street, Hull - what is now part of the city's student area. Mary was thin and frail and with gaunt facial features. She would have been about sixty at the time, but looked eighty plus, if she was alive today! People did in those days, look much older than they actually were, due to poorer living conditions, poorer health care and even a poorer diet. People were not appearance aware, then. Even the clothing was rather bland and mundane with less choice in the department stores. Ladies would have had their weekly 'shampoo and set' hairdo and then have worn a head scarf! Weird. Mary would come to our terraced property in Cottingham and the two of us would make our way on foot, along Endyke Lane (strangely spelt 'Endike' at the Hull end), pausing along the way to look at some pigs in a paddock and then turn right into New Village Road. Great aunt Mary and I then crossed over and entered 'the snicket', a long, fairly straight ginnel walkway with a panelled concrete wall all along the left side protecting the University of Hull grounds, still disused to this day, but recently the concrete fence has been replaced by a green wire one enabling pedestrians to view the derelict grounds therein. This snicket would take the two of us all the way to the east side of the station buildings of the Hull bound platform of Cottingham Station. But before we got there we would need to climb a gentle slope to reach the open ticket gate of the platform, passing round the back of the southbound waiting room and cycle shed.

Walking home one day along this snicket that lined a small brook, at about seven or eight years old after a trainspotting session, I discovered a small green tiny

DAVID KAY

Great Aunt Mary, Me & Aunt Norah.
I'd be aged 11 in 1964.

MEMORIES OF COTTINGHAM STATION

common frog along the snicket's path. Not knowing what I was about to do, being uninformed as I was alone, I would be taking my frog to its uncertain death by carrying it home in my hand and releasing it in our garden, unless it could find water quickly! Mother wasn't really interested in my misdemeanor, bringing a frog home, away from its environment.

As far as I can recall, all those sixty-two years ago, it was always spring or summer when great aunt Mary and I made these walks to Cottingham Station. We obviously never went in foul weather. We would then sit on one of the platform seats intended for waiting passengers. But in 1957, I don't recall many people about mid-morning. Although my first introduction to the wonderful world of railways was that year and most of the British public was still being carried by steam powered trains. Yorkshire had been chosen as one of the test areas for the introduction of what are called diesel multiple units or DMUs which had taken place on 7th.January that year, in Hull.

These new fangled trains would usually operate in multiples of two, four, six or eight cars when British Railways trains were really busy and seeing a three, five or seven car unit was completely unknown in their early years. Having said that, I have a dvd of heritage DMUs in East Yorkshire that even shows nine and ten car DMUs heading for Filey Holiday Camp with an unsightly mixture of lined green and BR blue stock in the consist! The DMUs had been built just recently from 1956 for use in this area by companies with long names like: Birmingham Railway Carriage & Wagon Manufacturing Company Limited, and a similar

Top: Gresley Streamlined Pacific, No.60019 "Bittern" heads north on a charter special.

Bottom: A Hull bound Cravens DMU at Cottingham with the addition of the cheesebox. It would now be about 1963.

MEMORIES OF COTTINGHAM STATION

sounding plant in Gloucester. There was Cravens in Sheffield that built such trains for the Hull area and used extensively on the Withernsea & Hornsea branches. Metropolitan Cammell also in Birmingham with their familiar rasping exhaust sounds, was another popular manufacturer at the time and had specialised in building Pullman carriages which I'll be discussing later. Even British Railways own Derby and Swindon works built their own brands, with the latter, my favourites running as dedicated six-car units with a buffet car on the Hull-Liverpool *Trans-Pennine* service usually taking three hours. (Sadly, no connection with the train operating company *Trans Pennine Express* of today). Sadly again, no *Trans-Pennine* units (now class 124, one carriage with or without engines) has been preserved for future generations to enjoy to reminisce with. The Birmingham RC&W company had also built a further lot of DMUs in 1961 which they referred to as Calder Valley units as they were intended for that route between Manchester and Bradford/Leeds via Halifax, following the route of the River Calder in West Yorkshire. The class 110s had a different end appearance to the class 104s, as they had a top, four-character headcode panel to display train reporting numbers for signalmens identification.

In actual fact, the very first experimental DMUs had been built in 1954, but only in smaller lots to an order with BR's Derby works. They were allocated to West Yorkshire, the Lake District and Northern Pennine rural areas and were never seen in Hull. The Derby lightweight class 108 twin sets were mainly allocated to rural services in Lincolnshire, so again were not seen on

The famous poster on Cottingham Station. "Ask the Man at Cooks...He knows", it said.

The terraced cottage on Thwaite Street where Aunt Mary used the outside toilet.
The side gate is new.

MEMORIES OF COTTINGHAM STATION

the Cottingham line, but would meet the New Holland, Humber ferry paddle steamers across the river at the pier station for trains to Cleethorpes and Barton-upon-Humber. And yes, Jonathan my brother and I did get this treat as well, but no further than the timbers of the pier station over the murky waters of the River Humber.

"Ask the Man at Cooks, he knows". Whilst aunty Mary and I were sat on the Hull-bound platform of Cottingham station, there would nearly always be an advertising poster on one of the platform's station building poster boards. We both wondered what all this was about. Naturally, when I was five, six or seven years old, I'd never heard of Thomas Cooks Worldwide Travel Service, then just known as 'Cooks'. This poster was a complete mystery to us at the time. There was this pleasing man's face and on one side of him was a long queue of globes or faces going round in a large crescent, covering the entire depth of the poster. We didn't bother reading the small print. Little did I know it then, but in 1970, I would myself become, 'The Man at Cooks', when the opportunity presented itself to me to work for that Worldwide travel chain. More about this later.

I can't remember how long great aunt Mary and I sat on the platform for, but I would imagine it wasn't longer than an hour and a half, at most. There were toilets across on the northbound platform, the Ladies being in a waiting room reserved specifically for the fairer sex, but Mary and I never ever ventured over the trusty footbridge connecting the two platforms. There was a barrow crossing at the Hull end of the platforms, but always a sign proclaiming **'Passengers must not cross the line except by means of the footbridge'**. The

A Birmingham unit arrives at Cottingham from Bridlington or Scarborough on a very wet afternoon.
Thanks to Hull Daily Mail for this photo taken in 1969.
The unit would be in plain blue.

barrow crossing, which used old railway sleepers, was there purely for the use of the station staff (more of which about, later) taking luggage, parcels and even baskets of racing pigeons from one platform to another. The reason I mention going to the toilet is that something rather bizarre happened on the way home, of which today would be completely unthinkable! Mary and I used to walk home along another route, taking in Station Walk (a driveway that parallels the railway line for some distance), turning left into Thwaite Street with its tiny crossing-gate box (more about this later, too). It

MEMORIES OF COTTINGHAM STATION

was in Thwaite Street, where, after crossing over the not very busy road (this makes me feel ancient!), we would call at the first, end terraced house of a Victorian/Edwardian block and unbelievably to a four year old, my great aunt would ask to use the lady owners outside toilet! Could you imagine that happening today in the 21st.Century? After she had relieved herself, we continued along Thwaite Street, negotiated the roundabout into Hull Road, crossed over and turned left into Inglemire Lane back home.

Getting back to Cottingham Station then. I can't remember how many trains we would wait for and watch as they all stopped. Only two trains a day didn't stop at Cottingham at all and I would later know this as a Cottingham trainspotter. Passing times: 9.26am, Scarborough-Hull express and non-stop from Driffield to Hull in twenty-five minutes. Almost unthinkable today, this four car train passing through George Townsend Andrews' wonderful trainshed at Beverley without stopping. In the northbound direction it was 5.16pm, Hull-Scarborough express (A4 headcode) but the latter, not on a Saturday. This was shown **SX** in timetables. This one did call at Beverley for Hull commuters. Today, all trains stop at Cottingham, including the *Hull Trains*, London Kings Cross-Beverley service first introduced on 4th.February 2015, and in both directions too, but the Cottingham stop would come later. Who would have thought fifty plus years ago, that one would be able to board and leave two trains a day at Cottingham and get off in the capital city, would become a reality one day. That certainly is progress! More about *Hull Trains* in the last chapter.

Top: A class 121 single car, Pressed Steel unit on the Wensleydale Railway at their Leyburn Station.
Bottom: The "Trans Pennine Express" DMU crosses Selby swing bridge into the platform there, on a Liverpool working.

MEMORIES OF COTTINGHAM STATION

CHAPTER 2
DIESEL MULTIPLE UNITS

All the new diesel trains were painted in the standard British Railways lined green livery which suited them well. On the front ends they had a 'cats whisker' as a warning sign to track workers and this was rather futile and would later be changed to a yellow rectangular warning panel, which we trainspotters would describe as a 'cheesebox' and all through the 1960s we referred to DMUs as cheeseboxes. When BR blue was introduced from 1965, this cheesebox would become an 'all yellow' cab front for even better sighting way down the track. Interrupting this cats whisker was a two-digit number panel. This carried roller blinds displaying numbers and letters. "A" would denote an express service, only stopping at Beverley, Driffield, Bridlington and Filey on the route we are discussing. "B" would indicate a stopping train calling at most stations along its route. So, B4 would show to signalmen that the approaching train was a Hull-Bridlington or Scarborough service or vice versa. B9 would be the local thirteen-minute run from Hull to Beverley and back and B5, a DMU on a York train. This latter service was withdrawn on 27th.November 1965 due to lack of use, under Doctor Beeching's infamous "Reshaping British Railways" plan of 1963.

DAVID KAY

There was a "C" I believe, but this was for parcels traffic only and was never witnessed by the author. British Railways (BR) contracted Gloucester Carriage & Wagon Company to build ten and Cravens of Sheffield to build three, purely DMU Parcel units. These were only for use around the conurbations of London, Birmingham and Manchester. So in the 1960s, I've only got three red underlinings in my last 1968 British Railways combined volume, which means I only witnessed three sightings of these unique DMU parcel cars, dating from 1959 & 1958 respectively. But more about trainspotting at Cottingham later on.

Today, all trains show very powerful LED lights in left and right hand clusters with red at the rear (and class 66 freight locos with a top headlight too). This means that the fifty-year old tradition of painting unit and engine fronts yellow is now being phased out for good. Track gangs can see high density lights much further away down the line than yellow panels.

So that was my introduction to trains and the world of railways which would last a lifetime and still does, but very sadly not access me a lifetime career working with them. In 1970 when I left school, the railways were in serious decline and all rolling stock was by then painted a drab blue colour and any positions available had to be through 'closed doors'. I'm sure readers will know what I mean. I wish not to dwell on this aspect of my life but was lucky enough to end up working for the world's best known travel agency chain and even selling British Railways 'Edmundson' card tickets for business travellers from a rack behind me at the counter at Thomas Cooks, as mentioned earlier. At least that was a

MEMORIES OF COTTINGHAM STATION

fantastic 'second best' to actually be working on the stations or trains themselves! Mary Camp, I have a lifetimes gratitude to thank her for, for introducing me to this fascinating subject and I wouldn't have asked for anything different!

I've just taken my seat immediately behind the small driving cab of the DMU. It's the best seat on the train and always was and a choice of five different positions too, to chose from. Three one side of the isle, two the other except in first class where it would be four and offering more space and comfort. You can still do this today to reminisce the old days of fifty and sixty years ago:-

Even on the just introduced Sheffield tram-train service, you can sit right at the front, but only in the two seats on the right hand side and look down the line as you travel from Rotherham Parkgate Shopping Centre to Cathedral tram stop in Sheffield city centre or the other way round. You will be able to watch everything the driver does, like open and close the doors and even see the speedo in clock and digital form. The driver has a centre seat here behind a locked glass door, but regrettably, the two left hand seats don't offer such a view. The entire journey, most of which runs on 'heavy rail', except in Sheffield city centre, takes 28 minutes and speeds of 50mph are briefly reached between Attercliffe and Arena/Don Valley Stadium stops (the latter demolished some years ago).

The best location though, is between Leeming Bar and Redmire on The Wensleydale Railway in North Yorkshire, who always have a DMU in operation when I go there. Its an 18 mile line running through extremely

A Thompson B1 No 61304 leaving Cottingham for Hull in 1948

The house at 12 Sands Lane, Bridlington that used to be 'Seacrest Boarding House' wh[ere] the Kay family stayed four ti[mes] in the 1950s and 60s.
(This was taken at dusk, befo[re] knew it would be included in book, one day).

MEMORIES OF COTTINGHAM STATION

rural and pleasing territory. Two intermediate towns of Bedale and Leyburn are worth exploring on route. On my last visit, it was one of the unique Pressed Steel built Class 121 'bubblecar' units. This means it's a single unit diesel railcar and operating alone, just like todays Class 153 units usually do. But they can be coupled up to other single units or make up a full DMU train but without interconnecting vestibules. Pressed Steel built sixteen of these cars in 1960 for very lightly and under-used branch lines, but alas, this wouldn't save them from the Beeching Axe.

Gloucester Railway Carriage & Wagon Company had previously built twenty single units in 1958 for the same purpose. They were all allocated to the London Midland and Western Regions of British Railways. Both types had sixty-five second class seats but no first. You can also travel on one of these class 122 solo units as I've just done on The Weardale Railway in County Durham, but I advise travellers to use their main station at Stanhope at the far end of their sixteen mile line. There are few parking spaces at Bishop Auckland Station (the train arrives 200 yards away at Bishop Auckland West) and its fatal to use nearby shoppers car parks due to time limit restrictions with cctv cameras watching you! A word of warning, though. You will only be able to ride on these class 121 & 122 single-car units in one direction only, sitting behind the driver. The other end contains the guards/luggage compartment, again with the detail that 1.5 tons of whatever may be carried, if evenly distributed.

And then there was a motley collection of lighter four-wheeled railbuses, but they only operated in really

Two 1958 German built railbuses in Haworth yard, Worth Valley Railway. These unique vehicles can still be seen there.

remote parts of England and Scotland and still didn't save the lines they were operating on, from closure. Two such examples were in Gloucestershire, were Kemble had two branches from the main line running south-west and north-east respectively, to Tetbury and Cirencester. They both closed on 6th.April 1964 due to lack of passengers and the motor car beginning to dominate the area by then, or even bus competition. Five were even built by a German company, Waggon & Maschinenbau of Donauworth in 1958. For British Railways then, this was totally unchartered territory only thirteen years after hostilities. I'm glad to report that all but one of this class have been preserved.

So, you had a comfy seat looking over the driver's shoulder on the left side of the train. You could sit on the

MEMORIES OF COTTINGHAM STATION

right side and not have a shoulder to look over, but if you were unlucky, in those days there might have been a co-driver or secondman with the driver. The other end of the two, three or four car DMU would have been first class only. If the train was the other way round, I would have to sit looking down the line through the empty cab. This wasn't half as much fun, seeing where you had already been! The engine under the floor would be ticking over and the train ready to depart. The driver's upper quadrant signals gave the all clear. The driver just had to wait for the double-buzz from the guards compartment and we're off. Today the conductor/guard has to sit in the rear cab when not checking tickets as there is no guards van as such, as there was in my day, on all trains. It's almost a thing of the past and consigned to history. You could always hear this distinctive buzz at the front of the carriage. One other memorable sound from the cab was the distinctive long, deep hiss when the driver applied the vacuum brake to slow the DMU down. And above all, let's not forget the lovely two-tone horn the driver would blow when he saw a 'Whistle' board by the trackside, unless there were animals near the track, or worse still pedestrians crossing where they shouldn't have been! So if nostalgia is your thing and you too, grew up with the DMUs like I did, get yourself off to The Wensleydale or Weardale Railways or seek out online or in a railway periodical, where the diesel galas are being held on one of Britain's wonderful heritage railways. Get yourself sat behind the driver and see for yourself what it was like to look forward over the driver's shoulder, if you don't remember those heady days of the fifties, sixties, seventies and eighties, when these 'first generation' sets were phased out. On the Sprinters & Pacers and more modern stock you just cannot do this. Their drivers are now screened-off in a locked cab.

You could never do the same on my favourite *Trans Pennine* Class 124, six-car DMU, as both motor composite driving units had a twenty-one seat, first class compartment behind the driver's cab, so this would have been totally impossible unless you forked-out for a first class ticket, which we could never afford then. Today, due to security issues, the driver is locked away in his cab without windows behind him. At night on the old units, the driver would pull down a blind behind him to eliminate any reflection of the passengers sitting behind him, so this had been a daylight treat only. It was similar too, on the old-style buses I grew up with, where the driver sat high-up in a cab on **his** own. Women bus drivers did not exist in those days!

Writing the last paragraph, has just reminded me of two tragic railway crashes that occured in the area covered by this book, but happily not whilst I was train spotting. The most recent one was at 1000hrs on 26th.July 1986 at Lockington, between Driffield and Beverley and involved a Bridlington to Hull working. The 0933 ex-Bridlington, passenger DMU hit a Ford Escort van on a level crossing. The train consist comprised a two-car Cravens Class 105 unit leading a two-car Class 114, Derby heavyweight unit. The crossing was completely 'open' to both road and rail users without any barriers or gates but the oncoming train had been protected by red flashing light signals which were working. The location had recently been

MEMORIES OF COTTINGHAM STATION

converted from traditional wooden gates, where the driver of any vehicle wishing to cross the line would have had to complete a lengthy process to cross. You left your vehicle and crossed the line on foot to the other side, checking for approaching trains either way. Open the far gate away from the track. Return to your vehicle and open the near gate, again away from the track, still checking the line. Quickly drive over the crossing. Get out your vehicle and repeat the process, starting with the far crossing once again. This could take upto five minutes. There had been 66 passengers on the Hull train that day, of which 37 were injured. There were nine fatalities in total.

On 14th.February 1927, on the track layout between Hull Paragon and West Parade signalboxes at 9.10am, steam trains from Withernsea (8.22) and the 9.05am to Scarborough collided head-on, but as this is not during the time scale of this book, I won't give any more details, suffice to say there were twelve deaths on that winter's morning. Both rail tragedies can be seen in full at: **wikipedia.org/wiki/Lockington_rail_crash & wikipedia.org/wiki/Hull_Paragon_rail_accident.**

Top: The staff of Cottingham Station around the turn of the 20th century
Bottom: A Beverley to Hull push-pull set in the Edwardian era. The loco is in the centre. This arrangement was only for short journeys

MEMORIES OF COTTINGHAM STATION

CHAPTER 3
COTTINGHAM STATION'S HISTORY

Cottingham railway station opened on 6th.October 1846 as part of the Hull & Bridlington line of the York & North Midland Railway and was built on a close of land known as the Boscroft. The Hull & Selby Railway Company had originally planned the line as a single track branch, who obtained the necessary Act of Parliament on 30th.June 1845. However on the following day, the company was leased perpetually to The York & North Midland, who took on the development. The builders of the line were Messrs Jackson & Bean and the engineer in charge was J.C.Birkenshaw from York. The station at Cottingham was designed by George Townsend Andrews (G.T.from now on), who was the architect for all the stations and buildings of the York & North Midland Railway, including York's original railway terminus and Hull Paragon. Cottingham Station originally consisted of one platform, a station master's house and a waiting room/ticket office. It was built of local brick as a single-storey building with bay windows and arched chimney stacks. The official opening train arrived at 11.20am and was met by cheering crowds. There was also a goods shed and coal depot. In 1868, a stone platform was constructed on the eastern side for passengers arriving from the New Village, which included another waiting room and later, a bicycle shed. Gas lighting wasn't introduced until 1902/3 and at the time the colour scheme was North Eastern 'chocolate & cream', to later become the remit of the Great Western Railway and the Pullman Car Company. A gents toilet was provided on the northbound platform near the footbridge, whereas the Ladies had their own waiting room on the same side. Both platforms eventually accomodated cycle sheds.

On 31st.July 1854, the line became part of the North Eastern Railway which was much later amalgamated to form the LNER in 1923 when the corporate colour scheme became green and cream. On New Years Day 1948 the railways were nationalized to form British Railways (BR) when Cottingham was part of the North Eastern Region and repainting once again became necessary to include tangerine as the main colour base. From 1965 this was shortened to British Rail and every window frame, running-in board*, totem plate, the footbridge and other miscellany became an all-over drab blue. Station signage would eventually be in white with black script. (*The running-in board was the main station nameplate. A totem plate was a smaller nameplate attached high up on lamp posts and repeated several times along the platform's length)

One of the most popular Cottingham Station employees was Harold Burton who worked there from 1926 until his retirement in 1966, where he undertook a variety of duties such as gatekeeper, ticket collector, cashier, cleaner, porter and shunter. He was also a very competent gardener and in the 1950s provided Cottingham Station with a vivid floral display in the

MEMORIES OF COTTINGHAM STATION

station gardens (now St.Mary's Mount flats, walking towards Beck Bank and Hallgate) and also maintained the flower garden beds along the platforms, as well as a number of hanging baskets around the station. I must say at this stage, that Cottingham station on many occasions would win 'best kept station award' for the North Eastern Regions' Hull area and the Divisional Manager would personally call in his private inspection saloon, attached to a Hull based 2-6-0 mogul from the Riddles-Standard 3 Class, more than likely No.77012. I have access to footage of this happening at Ferriby on the Hull mainline. I would have known Mr.Burton by sight in the 1960s, but obviously not known his name during these trainspotting years.

William Phillips is recorded as one of the earliest Cottingham Station masters in 1851, a role that would continue until 1972 when Francis J Watson would be the last incumbent at Station House. Robert Smith was probably one of the most active station masters, serving for 21 years at Cottingham, as well as undertaking his normal duties, he was also a successful gardener, which resulted in Cottingham winning prizes in 1902/3 for one of the best kept stations in the area as described above.

Goods traffic ceased in 1964, (after which time the sidings would later be dismantled and the entire site rationalized to the running lines only). BR had been fully privatized by 1997 and the line is now under the control of the train operating company Northern Rail, again with a standard blue colour scheme but brighter than British Rail blue. Their trains also incorporate purple into the livery carried and some include advertising vinyls.

Crabley Creek crossing near Brough. Saved from demolition due its use as a public right of way and farm access. Here, cows cross the line.

The 12.45 from Hull to Scarborough as shown in table 13 of the N.E.Region timetable. The reporting code for this train would have been A4.

16 London (King's Cross) dep		E pm	pm	H pm
HULL dep			12 45	
Cottingham arr	A		12 58	
Beverley dep			12 59	
Arram		Worcester (S.H.) dep 7.15 am		Liverpool (Ex.) dep 9.5 am
Lockington				
Hutton Cranswick				
Driffield arr			1 15	
Driffield dep			1 16	
Nafferton				
Lowthorpe				
Burton Agnes				
Carnaby				
Bridlington arr		1 24	1 33	1 50
Bridlington dep		1 29	1 38	1 55
Flamborough			1 46	
Bempton			1 51	
Speeton				
Hunmanby				
Filey Holiday Camp arr		1 52		
Filey dep			2 8	2 18
Filey			2 11	2 23
Gristhorpe				
Seamer				
SCARBOROUGH (C) Londesborough Road arr	B			2 37
Central			2 29	

MEMORIES OF COTTINGHAM STATION

As of 1891, the staff here included five clerks, three porters, two gatekeepers, three general railwaymen and three signalmen were occupied full time.(I can only think that gatekeepers would be responsible for manning crossing boxes). Wow, sixteen staff in the late nineteenth century! Other sources tell me that Cottingham had ten full time staff during the heyday of railway travel.

In 1988, Cottingham Railway Station, together with the adjacent goods shed became Grade ll listed status and both are now in private ownership with the latter being home to small businesses. Nowadays, although the station still retains a little charm, it is a shadow of it's former self and has been virtually unmanned since 1988. All the rooms and offices are boarded up for ever. There was a wooden platform extension facing northwards on the Hull-bound side during my tenure as trainspotter in the 1960s. In those days trains still carried more people from the coast than the roads did. Just! Trains were far longer then and needed the extra length for the disembarking hoards of day trippers! This extension has now long gone as most trains at the time of writing are still formed of two & three car units, except Hull Trains Beverley to London service, which is a five-car set.

The original footbridge still stands, although its rather forlorn now and needs replacing rather than repairs. There are however, large modern state-of-the-art ticket machines at both sides, which don't exist in the author's resident county of South Yorkshire on unmanned platforms. Even the train indicator boards are brand new and up to date. The semaphore signals have long been replaced with modern, colour light signalling which are now controlled from York Rail Operating Centre. Therefore the old traditional signal boxes, once a big feature of the railway landscape are now very few in number. I've just heard recently, that one at Crabley Creek on the Hull-Selby/Goole mainline near Brough, has to be retained because of ancient bylaws requiring gates to be opened for farm users and its also a little used public right of way, even during the night!

Cottingham station will always be there for its passengers, even though the station-based taxi office of modern times have now vacated their premises at the village side entrance. The railways of today are just functional. The charm, excitement and romance of train travel was left behind when the steam train disappeared in 1968. They will never be the same again. And one of the reasons I write this book is to evoke memories long gone.

MEMORIES OF COTTINGHAM STATION

CHAPTER 4
IT'S 1960
AND I'M OLD ENOUGH

I remember one June evening, watching my father laboriously extract information from the Summer timetable of that year and write it down in brief in a notebook, just for me, his eldest son. Dad had just walked out of his job at a shipping office in Hull's old town around this time. More about this later on.... I was about to start my ten year tenure as a trainspotter! Dad would have a selection of 'Bic' biro pens in four different colours: black, blue, green & red. As in those wonderful years during my childhood, which I will always remember with great fondness, Hull originating trains towards Cottingham, had four corresponding destinations: Beverley, Bridlington & Scarborough and also York, on a line that branched off north west at Beverely North signalbox on the main A1174 Hornsea road. This was just north of Beverley station but came after Cherry Tree crossing and its box. This line closed in 1965 as mentioned earlier.

Probably my fondest memory of Cottingham Station was one bright, spring or summer's morning. It was probably 1961 or 62. I was alone and usually on the southbound platform. A tinny little bell would ring on the wall of the station office opposite me, where the ticket office was and where the head of the station staff would have his office...the Station Master. The one in charge on every station, whether there were just two staff or fifty or more. The Station Master was the one who was always honoured and looked up to and always wore a peaked cap in later years.

After the bell rang, the observer would look either way, up or down the line. This may seem rather out of order, but it was always 'up trains to Hull' and 'down trains to Beverley and Bridlington'. This was because this was the direction of London. This obviously would right itself in the counties below London from Cornwall to Kent. This was railway parlance. It was always 'Up' trains towards London and 'Down' trains away from London. With one exception. The Manchester, Sheffield and Lincolnshire Railway, later to become the Great Central would defy this law and run trains their own way. The correct way round!

One would then observe a black smudge far down the line with a plume of white smoke emanating from above the black smudge. The smudge would get larger and larger and then before the 10.2am stopper from Bridlington reached Cottingham North crossing, (where New Village Road met Northgate), you would start to make out the outline of a steam locomotive heading towards the station platforms. The steam engine would be a tank locomotive carrying its water supply in large tanks either side of the boiler. It could also travel in either direction without the need for a turntable. This particular train would have originated at Bridlington and stopped at a string of wayside village stations with lovely sounding names like: Carnaby, Burton Agnes, Lowthorpe (all closed in 1969), Nafferton (still open),

MEMORIES OF COTTINGHAM STATION

then the market town of Driffield, before two more villages: Hutton Cranswick & Arram (the latter still open but not served by many trains now) and finally the market town of Beverley with it's magnificent G.T.Andrews built trainshed covering the tracks, before Cottingham, the last stop before Hull Paragon.

The 10.2am would screech to a halt under the footbridge. It was a Gresley designed V1 engine introduced in 1930 or a V3 rebuild from 1939 with higher boiler pressure. They had a pleasing 2-6-2 wheel arrangement and were classed as 3MT or 4MT, respectively. This was their power classification which ranged from 0 to 9. P for passenger engines, F for freight engines and MT represented Mixed Traffic locos. The V1/V3's weight was respectively either side of 85 tons but I won't bore readers with any more technical data. The specific engine hauling this train could be any of the following: 67635, 67638/40/63/77/82/84/86. These engines were allocated to 50B, Hull Dairycoates Shed by 1961/62 before being withdrawn for scrap. Previous to the change of the decade, this motive power depot (MPD) had been allocated as 53A and Botanic Gardens 53B, but things were already starting to be rationalised under British Railways Modernisation Plan of 1955. The Doctor, the infamous Richard Beeching had yet to arrive on the scene from ICI, in 1963 with his adventurous 'Reshaping the Railways' plan of that year!

Back to Cottingham Station on that beautiful unknown morning, in shall we say, 1961. I would hear the fireman stoking the firebox for the train's next and last eight minute leg to Hull. Steam trains always took a minute longer than DMUs due to their slower acceleration. The driver would be pottering about checking the controls and water level gauge as well as keeping a watchful eye on his side, awaiting the elevation of the 'Home' signal, a red rectangular plate with a white band 3/4 along its length. The signalman back in Cottingham North box would get the all clear from the next box (Thwaite Gates box, only controlled the road crossing gates), down at Cottingham South (mentioned later). The 'Home' arm would lift, the driver of the V3 would take the brake off, lift his regulator handle steadily, and after getting the whistle blown and green flag waved from the guard, probably towards the rear of the train, the six-coupled driving wheels would start the five or six coach medley of coaches and vans on its way towards Hull. The consist would mainly be Gresley and Thompson designed corridor coaches as this was the norm in the early days of British Railways. Standard mark one open saloon carriages **(TSOs),** were introduced in 1951 and even ten years later would still be reserved for the fastest expresses on the main lines and not a branch stopping train I am describing. The last coach, a **BCK** (brake corridor composite, first and second class) would pass the 'Home', it would drop to the horizontal once more, by which time our V3 would be over Thwaite Gates and the chuff-chuff-chuffing sound would gradually fade away and disappear as our 10.2am to Hull rounded the bend towards Snuff Mill Lane. I just regret I wasn't older and had camera to hand. But the memories will always be there. As far as I know, this could have been a return Bridlington working from much earlier that morning. I will never

MEMORIES OF COTTINGHAM STATION

know. Train crews would always work out and back on their roster's short routes. I have a Bachmann "00" scale model of what would become sister engine 67611, but in LNER lined black in my model collection as No.2911.

The A1 Steam Trust that built the fine Peppercorn A1 Pacific *Tornado*, completed in 2008, do have aspirations of building from scratch a new V3, once their current project with No.2007 *Prince of Wales* has been finished and even the following, mooted plan to build a Gresley K4 replica *Bantam Cock* sister engine, which they're going to number 3403 in the sequence. These projects take years to come to fruition, even if everything goes to plan! By this time I'll probably be a very old man, if I'm still alive! But at least they have set their projects well ahead. Since *Tornado,* the A1 Steam Trust have now seriously cut down the planning, CAD design and construction time scale of these new build projects. See **a1steam.com** for more details of the above.

What came as a massive surprise and a wonderful experience to my sheer amazement and delight, was that Cottingham would see many many special holiday excursion trains laid on to serve the thriving seaside resorts at Bridlington and Scarborough, not forgetting some even terminating at Butlin's holiday camp at Filey which had been opened in 1946 with three platform faces. These catered for the hoards of people then visiting holiday camps for their chalet holidays which were extremely popular at the time, before Continental air holidays took off in the late 1960s. A good proportion of these summer specials were steam hauled with many classes heading long trains of seven to thirteen carriages, either in BR maroon or the former 'blood & custard' colour scheme (mid red & cream) which was used for passenger stock from 1948 to 1956 and had not been repainted before the 1960s arrived, due to irregular servicing and maintenance.

The locomotives would then release themselves at the buffer points, before running tender first to Falsgrave depot at Scarborough, for servicing and turning for the evenings return, although there was a turning triangle connecting with the main line near this location. This would also mean running tender first, back to their waiting train at the holiday camp station at Filey. No station pilot was needed here as it was only operational at weekends.

What I was about to witness in 1960/1, mainly from Cottingham Station's Hull bound platform, was a constant stream of fabulous steam-hauled express passenger trains heading north, that at seven years of age, I really was way too young to fully appreciate. There were trains from the Lancashire cotton mill towns (although Blackpool and Morecambe were much closer, many holiday-makers preferred the East Coast resorts). There were trains from the Midlands and Chesterfield, from Sheffield, Rotherham and Doncaster. Trains from the West Yorkshire woollen mill towns. You name it, there was a train heading from there to Brid, Butlin's at Filey and Scarborough. I was mesmerized. Amid all this activity, the two level crossing gates at Cottingham: Thwaite Gates and Cottingham North still had to close to road traffic to let the regular scheduled stopping trains through as well, in between all the summer

MEMORIES OF COTTINGHAM STATION

specials. In those heady days of the early 1960s, those two railway tracks, which nearly closed years later, were extremely busy and Cottingham was more akin to a main line station. I pity the poor motorists having to wait for long periods at the road crossings when the gates would be closed to road traffic possibly longer than being open.

In 1960, three in every four summer excursion specials would still be steam powered. In numerical sequence, I witnessed LMS 'Crabs' (a 2-6-0 mogul that got this nickname because of its high running plates), Ivatt moguls, Stanier Black 5s, possibly my first ever named Royal Scot and Patriot classes. I will never know. Like an idiot, I did not keep my notebooks and Ian Allan ABC's in those days, except for the very last one of the latter containing steam in 1968. When a new edition arrived, all my numbers would get transferred with my brother's help and the old ABC actually destroyed! What foolish action. But we didn't know any better as children/teenagers! I wouldn't realise how vitally important reference books they would become in later years. But I did keep my last Ian Allan ABC combined volume from 1968. But the steam listings are quite small by this, the last year of steam on British Rail. I also have a repurchased copy of the very last ever Ian Allan ABC of Steam Locomotives. This came out in April 1965.

I would have to wait until 2015 to actually see 46100 *Royal Scot* in the flesh. Stanier also produced green LMS Jubilee's or 'Jubes' as we trainspotters nicknamed them (more about this class later). The LNER was represented by Gresley V2s, Thompson B1s, Raven

DAVID KAY

B16s and Gresley K3 & K1 classes, traditionally freight engines, though. Steam-allocated sheds would scramble anything they could find to get holidaymakers to the seaside for their annual, well-earned weeks holiday. Even if a passenger loco wasn't available, a freight engine would stand-in. Rather like the war effort, if it steamed, it would run on a summer special to Bridlington, Filey Holiday Camp or Scarborough.

The reason for this proliferation of steam power being used, was that diesel locomotives were still in their infancy at the end of the 1950s. Not many were yet in service. Mainly the Class 40 & 44-46 'Peaks' of today, what we called English Electric Type 4s and The Peak Class, respectively. These were the most powerful diesels of their day and came out the plants in 1958 & 1959. If you know about railways, you'll know that the Peak class were so called, as D1 to D10 were all named after English & Welsh mountains. Some other Peak diesels were named after regiments, scattered throughout the 193 strong class. There were also the lower powered engines being introduced in 1958 and 1957, the Sulzers and Brush Twos (classes 24 & 31), respectively. I fondly remember arriving at the station via Station Walk and seeing a double-header Brush Two passing through on a lengthy Chesterfield to Bridlington excursion shortly after half past nine in the morning.

I would stay and trainspot until after 1pm, the intensity of the trains was so great. And they would rush through Cottingham at upto 60mph, whereas today I believe there is a 20mph permanent speed restriction in force. Heaven knows why. All other classes of diesel

MEMORIES OF COTTINGHAM STATION

power would come later during the 1960s, as the day of the steam loco was gradually being phased out - slow at first. Then the pace got quicker and quicker and finally finished in 1968. But the rest of that story can be found in other books.

Whilst I was still very young and we knew a steam train was approaching the station, we loved nothing more than to climb the footbridge steps and get 'steamed out' as we called it. Allowing the steam loco to run under our feet and let its smoke envelope us. As it approached our view, all we would see, was the smokebox numberplate, so we knew which engine it was, hauling its train. But as we got older, we realised this was rather a childish activity and we were missing seeing anything but the engine's roof, coal in the tender and carriage rooftops.

The oven vent caps of restaurant cars with a kitchen **(RKO)** in the consist was a rare sight at Cottingham but yes, there were restaurant cars on the longer services in the high summer months, which meant people could be dining as these prestigious trains passed through. So eventually this practice ceased and we trainspotted sensibly from the platforms below. But it was great fun while it lasted.

Once apon a time, holiday specials avoided Cottingham and the coast line altogether and joined the route to the resorts at Driffield. They used the Selby & Driffield Railway until the late 1950s travelling via Market Weighton, but this line was purposely being run down as it carried very little regular traffic, there were no intermediate stations as they'd all previously been long-since closed and above all, the Selby & Driffield

DAVID KAY

Railway contained steep gradients over the Yorkshire Wolds, some so steep that double-heading was essential. Now this wasn't conducive to being efficient. So this line finally closed to all traffic on 14th.June 1965 and all excursions diverted via the Cottingham line.

So a plan was devised to route these summer specials through the outskirts of Hull. They would leave the main line at Dairycoates/Hessle Road crossing (Hull's first flyover opened in 1962) and head north over crossings and bridges at Boothferry Road, Anlaby Road and Spring Bank West, before connecting with the Cottingham line at Cottingham South Junction, which surprisingly was two miles down the line, south of what is now County Road flyover (not then built), opposite the Ideal Standard/Stelrad works of today. Later on, during the 1960s, even this line had to close.

Hull was notorious for the number of its road level crossings causing inconvenience to a growing number of motorists, but still only a fraction of the volume we see today. So this line closed and our lengthy summer excursion trains came even closer to Hull Paragon, when a new spur was installed at what was then the Oval cricket ground on Anlaby Road. Our trains would dive under the newly built (1964) Anlaby Road flyover and then branch left to squeal round the tight curve of where Hull's KComm Stadium now sits to join the Cottingham line and passing the then carriage depot before Walton Street level crossing.

As we all know, car is now king and always will be. People do not want the inconvenience of making a journey in segments. Walk or bus or get a lift to the

MEMORIES OF COTTINGHAM STATION

railway station to go on their holidays. Then get the train. Then get a taxi, bus or walk to their guest house or hotel. But when I was a child, we stayed at a boarding house in Bridlington, where full board (all meals) was included in the price. My parents never had a car and my father never drove. We couldn't even afford to stay at *The Seacrest* at No.12 Sands Lane every year either, but probably only went there four times during me and my brother's childhood.

    I must tell you how we usually got there. There were buses to town, but no, Dad would usually treat us to a booked taxi ride in an old TX3 London cab from Paragon Station, run by the Richardson company. They used to have an open platform next to the driver, where your suitcases were strapped in. Any excess luggage would be sat on the boot tailgate, as this was only small. Again, it would be strapped secure. The train we caught was a four car Birmingham RC&W, DMU leaving Hull Paragon about 11.15am (why we went that early, heaven knows.) Our train didn't run in the winter, so I do not have exact timings to hand. My brother and I were delighted as the train sped right through Cottingham without stopping and did so every summer Saturday morning. As our express DMU passed Carnaby airfield just before reaching its destination, my father would always take great delight in pointing out to his family the small row of missile rockets we could just see in the distance. The train would only stop at Beverley and Driffield and then we would leave Bridlington station in another taxi? No, we didn't. We would walk to the Promenade with our suitcases and eat our packed lunch which always included hard-boiled eggs, before proceeding to our accomodation to check in with our landlady, Mrs.Strefford. The week's annual holiday in bright, bracing Bridlington had begun!

So as more and more people bought cars to help them get to their holiday destinations quicker and more efficiently, the number of holiday excursion trains got less and less and by the late 1970s/early 1980s there just wasn't the custom about, so summer special excursion trains fizzled out and became a thing of the past. Filey holiday camp station platforms closed down in 1977 as trade had by then dwindled to such a low level. But don't despair, you can still travel by train to your chosen seaside resort, but Filey passengers do have a G.T.Andrews designed trainshed in which to disembark. But it'll just be a regular, scheduled two/three car service run for shoppers and day trippers and maybe people going to work on the late shift by todays *Northern Rail* company. And it most certainly won't have a special locomotive at the front, either - almost all trains today are formed of multiple units, even on our main lines travelling at 125mph!

There was myself, sometimes my younger brother Jonathan, Gordon my best pal, sometimes his younger brother Ramsay. Paul and Richard from Hymers College, not the local Cottingham schools, and sometimes even Francis in my class. At one point very briefly, an older girl called Christine joined us. She was a redhead and a right bitch to get on with. Why she was interested in trains, heaven knows. We were all of the same age group and born 1952-1955. So quite a crowd, but sometimes just the two or three of us. And later on, as you will read about other places, I was quite alone.

MEMORIES OF COTTINGHAM STATION

We would sit quietly between trains in the cold Hull-side waiting room in the winter months where the porters would have made a coal fire, but if you remember those, they took ages to get the room warmed up and then had to be roaring fires before the heat could be felt. We would have a railway quiz between ourselves. One would call out the names or number of locomotives listed in Ian Allan ABCs, and others would have to answer the question. I'll give you an example. A Gresley A4 Pacific loco no.60034. What name does this engine carry? The answer would be *'Lord Faringdon'*. Or, from the same class, the question the other way round. What number does the engine *'Merlin'* carry? The expected answer would be 60027. Sir Nigel Gresley's iconic, streamlined A4 Class, some of which carried names of birds, as it's been said Gresley just loved ducks and others were named after directors of the London and Northern Eastern Railway, including himself! There was one even named after a previous President of the United States: Dwight D.Eisenhower, which is preserved and was repatriated back to Britain in 2012-2014 for the 75th.anniversary of *'Mallard'* breaking the World Speed Record for steam traction of 126mph (just) on Sunday afternoon 3rd.July 1938 at 4.22pm on Stoke bank heading south, but thats another story and can be read elsewhere.

This event was known as "The Great Gathering" and was an exhibition of the six remaining (out of the 35 A4s built - one got obliterated by a bomb in 1941 that dropped on York North shed during the blitz - now the NRM), Gresley A4s and shown at the National Railway Museum at York and their outpost at Shildon, County

Durham. It was a sight no railway enthusiast would have missed.

Sometimes, our little quiz involved shed codes where the 'quizmaster' asked a shed code like 50B and the answer was Hull Dairycoates, but this is just a terribly easy example and we mainly avoided the easy ones. Ian Allan even produced an ABC book of shedcodes, which not only showed the entire shedcode listing from 1A Willesden, NW London to 89C Machynlleth with five sub sheds covering mid to north Wales, but also the shed allocation of every locomotive then in operation on the entire British Railways system. I won't bother listing any more, but you get the idea. These are quoted from the 1956/57 ABC British Railways Locomotives combined volume, but by 1968, the last year of steam operations, the last listing was 87E Landore shed at Swansea as coverage somewhat contracted, albeit slowly.

Things were very different during what we thought was then, the long hot dry and to us, never ending summer months. There could be up to six or seven of us. Kids as you know, are not quiet for long, particularly were boys are concerned. We could be sat on the LNER seat at the south end of the Hull-bound platform making a noise amongst ourselves. This would annoy the station staff as our behaviour wasn't conducive to running a train service and showing a bad example to any nearby passengers. We were asked to leave the station premises, not once, not twice but on a regular basis. Even the porters had the authority to do this. The station staff must have got hopelessly sick and tired of us over a period of time. Where would we go and carry on our

MEMORIES OF COTTINGHAM STATION

trainspotting activities? I'm going to cover the various haunts we had to visit to continue our hobby. The locations may not be in order as I'm only using my memory as I write. We're talking over fifty years ago! These were the early days of the 1960s.

At the top end of the goods yard where the weekday morning shunt took place, there was an old disused cattle ramp. It had a cinder and gravel slope at it's southern end and was surrounded with wooden fencing. At the back of the cattle ramp was the access road to Paley & Donkin's carpet factory. The goods yard itself was accessed from Beck Bank/Hallgate junction in the village. This was the ideal place to trainspot if we'd been asked to leave the station platforms. It gave an excellent, all round and clear view of every train that passed. We also had hearing range of the activities within Cottingham North level crossing signalbox (see below). We could hear the bell codes being received from Beverley Park Gates box, three miles to the north, for a Hull-bound train, so knew when the signalman was going to close the gates to road traffic. This was long before lifting barriers were installed and the gates I remember were mainly long, low-profile wooden gates, supported by thick, small rubber tyres sweeping across the road when they closed. They could be described as 'ahead of their time'. This is what I remember from my days as a trainspotter, upto sixty years ago.

Cottingham North Box was disconnected and 'taken out' from the network over the weekend of 21st/22nd.November 1987. It was destined to be preserved in a museum in Hull and the roof was

DAVID KAY

Two of the ill-fated class 14 Paxman diesel hydraulics, double-head a cross city freight through Botanic Gardens station.

MEMORIES OF COTTINGHAM STATION

removed and taken by lorry to Wilmington Bridge on the River Hull for transport by barge to the Hull Museums High Street warehouse, where it would eventually be put back on the signalbox cabin for display. This 'Cottingham North' box had replaced an earlier box on the other side of Northgate, dating from 1874. Barriers would now be installed and controlled from Beverley. These modern, low profile gates I remember (as above), were propelled by electric toe motors, with each of the four gates having its own motor and would become the first in the Hull area to be so equipped, followed shortly by Walton Street crossing, just a mile from the buffers at Hull Paragon station, where we shall be going later on. You may still visit Cottingham North crossing box and go inside to see the signal lever frame in *Hull's Street Life Museum* in the High Street of the Old Town. The original rod-operated gates are preserved there too.

For over a century, the main business at Cottingham was freight. I knew that coal and coke were handled as I witnessed this traffic, together with imported timber and livestock (due to this long-disused animal access ramp) and newspapers offloaded at the passenger platform, as described later. The following long-lost trade comes as a complete surprise therefore:- grain, stone, tar and believe it or not, Hull's human and animal excrement, to fertilise local market garden produce to return to Hull markets for sale, c.1908. There were ten station staff at the time. Today, all these trades are no more and Cottingham goods yard comprises an endless stream of small local businesses of all descriptions with *Stoneledge*, a contract hire business being of some standing. The ambience I once remember is sadly, no more and never will exist again. Even the 1960's built Danish Bacon factory has been demolished to make way for new developments.

Snuff Mill Lane kissing gate crossing was another haunt we could have visited when we'd got thrown off the station for our rowdy behavior. Snuff Mill Crossing didn't actually give any good vantage points and had quite restricted views to approaching trains as one had to keep back from the fences there. Just south of Snuff Mill Crossing on the east side of the Beverley-Hull railway line was an embankment. This feature had been built before World War 2, with a view to constructing a flyover there for road traffic. After hostilities, construction never continued and the un-named hill was just the ideal alternative spot from which to trainspot as we were twenty feet above the tracks and excellent views were again commanded in both directions. After nearly thirty years of disuse, naturally this proposed road was by then grassed over and with foliage and tussocks and even trees were wildly growing in places, but access was good. Coming away from the end of Bricknell Avenue, access is by the side of Cottingham Croxby Primary School and is still available to this day. But strangely enough, I seem to remember only being here alone!

Another location that was inhabited by possibly just me and Gordon was the goods shed. For this we had to trespass as we needed to sit on the large concrete slabs that formed the loading bays for the Continental ferry vans, and then only if that siding was clear of rolling stock. Below our dangling legs was a railway siding.

You can still see a Hughes-Fowler 'Crab' freight engine. This is the doyen of the class, No.2700 in the Station Hall at the NRM, York in express passenger, crimson lake.

One of the stalwarts of the Worth Valley Railway on a passenger service at the Bronte village of Haworth on the West Riding's five-mile tourist line. 90733 was built as a hard-working WD freight engine for the Ministry of War Supply in 1945.

Preserved WD Austerity, No 90733 masquerades as work-stained No. 90711 classmate, on a demonstration goods train on the Worth Valley Railway out of Keighley, West Yorkshire.

The British Railways 'cycling lion' logo as found on a diesel multiple unit before 1966.

The very last Ian Allan ABC spotters book to contain steam locomotives. This dates from 1965. A Thompson A2 Pacific loco graces the cover.

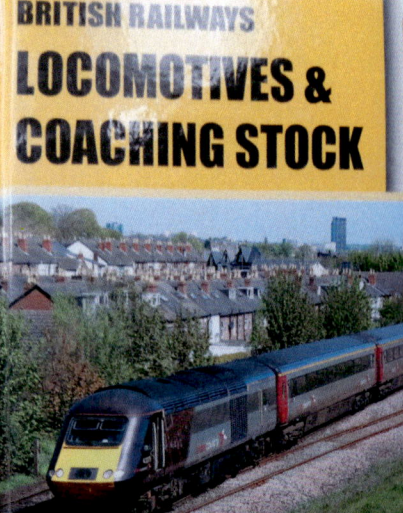

Platform 5's 2015 Combined Volu of Locomotives and Coaching Sto in Great Britain. This will be the author's last random copy.

MEMORIES OF COTTINGHAM STATION

The goods shed had two large arches either side, one for rail traffic and the far side for lorries to pull up. The main use of the shed was timber, one of only two commodities being handled at Cottingham by 1960, the other being coal. This spot would again have great views up and down the line. But we didn't inhabit here much. I do recall being sat there one wet, miserable Saturday afternoon and watching a Hughes/Fowler Crab, 2-6-0 goods engine pass in the Hull direction on a homeward-bound summer holiday extra returning weekly train to Leicester, or some such other exotic destination with a rake of Midland (LMS) designed stock from the 1930s. In the heady days of the 1960s, there was a terrific amount of variety on the railways in the rolling stock, the locomotives used and types of trains run. The Freight, 'Crab' loco would have been scrambled for operation due to no passenger loco being available at the shed that morning.

Our last chosen trainspotting outpost of the mid to late 1960s was one I would never have chosen in a million years! It gave very little viewing opportunity and was on a small hilly mound by the side of Thwaite Gates crossing box, which was across the road to us. We didn't see any train until it came out from behind the box and then as quickly disappeared behind a large advertising billboard where we were or vice versa. We only saw the trains run through the gates and that was it! There was a 'Home Starter' signal behind the billboard and I remember once there being a summer excursion train halted here for some time as there'd been a derailment near Driffield, twenty miles towards Bridlington. It was headed by a class 31, Brush Type 2

Riddles Standard 3MT No.77012 with a Divisional Managers inspection saloon, as discussed in the text, for awarding 'Best kept station' prizes.

WDs at rest in their home shed, 50B Hull Dairycoates roundhouse, facing the turntable.

MEMORIES OF COTTINGHAM STATION

diesel. There was also a phone box just fifteen yards away towards Snuff Mill Lane. It was in the standard, Hull Corporation green & cream livery and was square with a pinnacled top. But we were finally on the street and out of trouble, albeit with severely reduced visibility. This signal cabin did not have any signals to control. The gateman just had to wait for a gap in the traffic, which usually wasn't very long in those days. There were no flashing lights or loud claxons to immediately stop traffic. The gates would swing out into the road in two sections, wound by a large ships-type wheel from the cabin. The side gates to pedestrians would also lock shut. There was just a large red wooden circle in the middle of the gate to denote Stop! Things were very primitive then compared with today. We didn't know what the future had in store. There wasn't even an emergency telephone by the gates...we didn't need one. The gateman would be keeping a careful watch on proceedings from his box window. This latest trainspotting post of ours, had originally been the pitch of a cannon siting from 1904 to the 1930s and had been used in the Boer War. It was removed then, due to safety issues as was a duplicate on West Green in the village, outside the Blue Bell Inn.

 I would arrive at our Thwaite Gates spot on foot to be provided with a list of jottings that would include train reporting numbers (headcodes), destinations returning from the coast resorts and times of passing Cottingham. Our Hymers' friends, Richard or Paul had been to have a chat with the gateman in his cabin to obtain this very useful information, which was as always, pretty much accurate. There were no regular

DAVID KAY

Sunday bookings then, only the normal scheduled stopping trains. The returning summer excursion specials would have come up to Bridlington and Scarborough that morning. (Remember that trains to Filey were only servicing Butlins Holiday Camp and didn't go just for the day). On a quiet Sunday and with lousy weather, there was maybe only four or five returning extras to the usual places mentioned earlier. On a busy weekend like a Bank Holiday Sunday or Monday, this number might even stretch to fifteen extras or more. It was now the 1965-1968 period and even then, things were starting to slow down slightly on the excursion front. We had no interest in local trains rapidly changing colour from lined green into plain blue. And from the attractive British Railways 'cycling lion' logo to a plain white double arrow. How boring!

It was earlier that decade, when uncle Ron was bringing us back from a late afternoon mystery car outing that was the norm for many Sunday afternoons and Bank Holidays in the summer, when we were approaching Thwaite Gates crossing and they were closed against us. The train that shot across our limited view was a brunswick green Royal Scot class steam locomotive heading towards Hull. Or was it? I will never ever know if THAT WAS my first ever sighting of a Stanier rebuilt, Royal Scot. I would have to wait until 2015 to actually witness No.46100 *Royal Scot* outside the NRM at York as I passed by on a train and would later see it properly on the North Yorkshire Moors Railway at Grosmont. My uncle remarked that it could have been a diverted Glasgow to Nottingham express or something like that. I don't think so, at all. He knew

MEMORIES OF COTTINGHAM STATION

little about railways but did once provide me with a couple of interesting books about railways immediately after the war, he no longer wanted.

I cannot remember what year it was, but probably later during that glorious decade whilst I was growing up fast as a teenager. Don't ask me how I found out about this, but I got wind, that a pop-star would be aboard a specific, run of the mill DMU heading for Bridlington! It would have been a Friday or Saturday evening before teatime (6pm) and this black female singer was performing at the Bridlington Spa Theatre that very night, or if it was a Friday, possibly both nights or even the Sunday as well. Yes, you've guessed it. She was the 'one hit wonder', Millie, or Millicent Green, her full name with the big hit "My Boy Lollipop". I arrived on the up, Hull-bound platform to see Millie with her male agent and entourage in the front first class compartment of two, two-car class 105 Cravens units, across on the other platform. These still formed the majority of Beverley & Bridlington trains throughout my trainspotting years. I remember just walking to the station to see Millie and was glad I had done. I today believe in grabbing every single opportunity that life throws at you. You may not get another chance!

In 1969, Peter Sarstedt had a top-twenty hit about 'one more frozen orange juice'. In the years before 1969, we used to leave our Thwaite Gates trainspotting post for a few minutes and nip round the corner into a road called Beck Bank and head into a dinky cottage shop run by a Granny Smith? It still exists as Beck Cottage. Obviously we would time our escapes carefully and not go when we knew a summer excursion train was due.

DAVID KAY

We didn't want to miss anything important. The purpose of this shopping trip was to buy ourselves a frozen orange juice called a 'Jubbly'. We loved them and they also came in blackcurrant but orange flavour was far more popular. You had to tear off the corner and then tilt the Jubbly above your head in order to drink the juice flowing off the frozen block of flavoured ice as it defrosted in your hands. They were a peculiar shape of which the likes I've never seen since. Apparently, Jubblys are still available.

It was the mid 1960s and our little group on the small mound behind the billboard hoarding were just waiting for one last 'morning' summer extra from London Kings Cross, no less. I say morning, as it was by now after 1pm! There were a few last trains taking holidaymakers home during the afternoon. The reporting code was something like *1F39* or *1G39*. All the Summer, regular excursion trains used the code letter 'F' or 'G', which seemed to alternate from year to year. It would pass Thwaite Gates cabin (not a signalbox, as it didn't control any signals) at about 1.15pm and was headed for Butlin's Filey Holiday Camp station. And do you know, I don't think the consist even included a buffet car and the journey would have been five hours in total! It would be 'hauled' by my favourite diesel locomotive, the class 47 - Brush 4, of which Brush works at Loughborough eventually built 512, the largest main line diesel class then on British Rail metals. They had 12-cylinder *Sulzer* engines of 2750bhp making them a powerful contender for the ECML *Deltic* class. I believe their transmission was by Hawker-Siddeley, where Dad worked drawing aircraft parts and spares, at Brough.

MEMORIES OF COTTINGHAM STATION

There was a connection, as one edition of that works house magazine that Dad brought home for me, had just that locomotive doyen on the cover. Yes, No.D1500 on the cover of an aircraft works magazine! I seem to remember also, the experimental 4000bhp loco *Kestrel* produced in 1968 by Brush and Hawker Siddeley in a garish yellow and brown livery, also featured at some stage on the cover of the same house magazine.

Hull Rag Week. Whats this all about you may ask. Thwaite Street in Cottingham, just happened to be along the route of a parade on the middle Saturday in June every year, at the time. Hull University halls of residence were nearby and the students had been getting ready all morning, dressing up in fancy clothes and decorating in all manners of fashion, their lorry floats that would carry them to their afternoon jamboree at the Hull University campus on Cottingham Road, a couple of miles away. Don't forget, readers who are old enough, will remember this was *The Age of Carnaby Street and the Swinging Sixties!* We were enthralled in the entire parade as it made its way out of Cottingham and sections obviously kept getting held up for the passing of still, a busy Saturday lunchtime train service. The students were excited and getting in the party mood - they were heading towards their Summer recess - a long three months away from their gruelling studies. At least us trainspotters saw some of the party parade on its way those years we inhabited our Thwaite Gates crossing post.

It was one lovely, pleasant summer Saturday evening. (Google tells me it was 1963 as this date in 1962 had been a Friday). I'd been to Steven's

DAVID KAY

10th.birthday party at his house in Cottingham. Steven was not into trains at all. His father was driving a few of us back home afterwards. Possibly a Morris Traveller. Francis had just been dropped off as his family were market gardeners on Dunswell Road or the North Moor Lane area. Cottingham North gates were closed to road traffic as we came out of Dunswell Road, so were lucky enough in getting a completely clear run into New Village Road by the ancient green and cream phone box, I remember being on that corner. What was even more amazing was just at that precise moment a steam hauled Saturday extra from Bridlington or Scarborough (Filey holiday campers would have gone back that morning after checking out of their chalets), dashed across the closed crossing. I recognised that engine, even through its filthy coat of layer apon layer of black grime and grease. This unknown express engine would have been a gorgeous lined brunswick green underneath that filthy black coat. Even in 1963, steam engines were being run down and neglected, not cared for or even cleaned regularly at their depots, overnight. This express engine certainly looked bigger than a Gresley V2, which itself would have been a highly unusual sight at Cottingham. But it very well could have been a V2 as they were mixed traffic engines and could be allocated to any type of work, even main line expresses. The train was travelling fast, as they could do in those days. The engine was that dirty, I couldn't even see any of the five, large white decals on the cabside displaying its running number! I couldn't even see that it had a name (this was rare at Cottingham) on a curved plate over the middle splasher. I would have to wait until the following night

MEMORIES OF COTTINGHAM STATION

until I met up with Richard or Paul, the Hymers' boys, who would be able to tell me what this namer had been.

On hearing what Richard or Paul had to relate, I was completely taken aback, blown away and flabbergasted. This sort of railway icon was just never seen on the coast line, but I just had to take the Hymers lads word for it and believe him. That Saturday evening, coming out of Dunswell Road from the window of Steven Larvin's fathers car, I had only witnessed a Gresley A3 racehorse hadn't I, in disgusting external condition. It had been *Firdaussi,* No.60038 and a sister engine to Alan Pegler's *Old Girl* (as he called her), 60103 *Flying Scotsman,* which the Retford businessman would have bought direct from British Railways that January. In fact, *Flying Scotsman* running as 4472 and in pristine lined apple green livery would be seen by me six years later after the finish of steam on the railways of Britain. 4472 was the ONLY exception to BRs ruling. I would pick the best vantage point at the top end of Cottingham yard, just before Cottingham North crossing to witness the world's most famous steam engine heading for Scarborough on a charter train.

I just couldn't believe what I'd just been told. An A3 through Cott with a holiday extra! Even to this day, nearly sixty years on, I wish I'd seen 60038 *Firdaussi* in 'full flight' from a proper vantage point and taken this magnificent occasion in, to the full. This was the one and only Gresley A3 that I ever spotted in normal everyday traffic. We were still well too young to have cameras and to be able to get to Doncaster or York without parental supervision! Just my luck. My motto is: I was born way too late to be able to enjoy the steam

Top: D6732, a one time 50B Hull Dairycoates engine, as seen at Weybourne on the North Norfolk Railway.

Bottom: Trans Pennine in its early lined green livery when introduced in 1960. This train never had the 'cats whiskers' applied.

MEMORIES OF COTTINGHAM STATION

scene, fully. And really appreciate it!

Nigel Gresley (later, Sir) had introduced his iconic A1 class in 1927 after showing off No.1470 *Great Northern* at the Empire Exhibition in 1924. After reconfiguring some of the class into A10s, they became the A3 in the end. Many A3s were named after racehorses as thats what they did: race up and down the East Coast Main Line with express passenger trains. 60038 was one of the early numbered examples, the class running from 60035 to 60112.

Firdaussi, the British thoroughbred racehorse and sire was born in 1929. He showed good form as a two year old when he won three of his five races, including the Dewhurst Stakes. *Firdaussi* was owned by none other than the Third Aga Khan! He was retired sometime after 1944. (Once again, thanks to Google for that information.) I'm pleased to say that *Firdaussi* the engine was not cut up by Albert Draper's team (of which more about later), although eight sister, racehorse-named examples were in 1964 & 1965.

In 1960 to 1964, I was at Cottingham Hallgate Juniors and would get the dedicated EYMS bus home or walk through some snickets by the side of the Junior Girls School (we were seperated in those days after the infants), and over some little bridges crossing Cottingham Beck and into the goods yard, passing the newly-built Danish Bacon Factory on the way. I must have carried my A6 feint-ruled notebook and possibly an Ian Allan ABC of Diesel Multiple Units with me, but cannot remember the latter being in my satchel as a permanent fixture. It was coming upto 3.45pm and the most important stopping train of the day was due to call at Cottingham's northbound platform, shortly. This was no special train hauled by a locomotive or anything like that. We're just talking about an everyday Birmingham RC&W Company built (class 104 in todays parlance), four-car DMU. The 3.45pm, Hull-Scarborough (shown in the 1963/4 NE Region timetable), calling at Cottingham naturally, Beverley, Driffield, Nafferton, Bridlington and then all stations to Scarborough. It would take ninety-one minutes for the 54 mile journey arriving at 5.16pm. What was so special about this particular, mundane DMU service? Without the running of this train, the people of East Yorkshire would go hungry. Not hungry for food, but hungry for the day's local news. Yes, the 3.52pm from Cottingham heading north was the all important mail train, not carrying the post, but the latest editions of *Hull Daily Mail,* the local evening press.

   Three or four, maybe five village newsagents would arrive in their cars outside the station gates and wait on the northbound platform for the 3.52's arrival. One of these newsagents was a Mr.Clifford, a resident of our street at the time, until the Lindstrom family bought No.21. With his dark rimmed sunglasses on, Mr.Clifford would remind me of the late American rock & soul singer, Roy Orbison. He also wore a black, open-necked shirt and had black, brylcreem'd hair, too. Almost a spitting image of the legend singer!

   After the DMU had pulled up at the platform, the newsagents would direct themselves towards the guards van part of the trailer brake second **(TBS),** as it was known, being the second or third coach. This would identify that a 1.5 tons load could be carried, if

MEMORIES OF COTTINGHAM STATION

distributed evenly. They would either collect a couple of large, stringed-up bundles of *Hull Daily Mail*, or perhaps put more bundles onto a platform trolley to cart away to their waiting cars outside. This train naturally ran every day except Sundays to supply the populace with their evening read. I would imagine that the *HDM* would be offloaded by newsagents similarly, at all the stations the train stopped at, but not after Bridlington. Any further, was really too far away to be of any good for this papers coverage and would arrive too late that evening, anyway.

   I still did not want to leave Cottingham Station after the 3.52pm paper train had left for Beverley. I stayed on. I would witness another six trains heading north before Dad arrived from work, including the 5.16pm non-stopper to Scarborough which only stopped at the main stations of Beverley, Driffield, Bridlington, and Filey, doing the journey in a reasonable 78 minutes. This really was the express service for Hull commuters and would show **A4** on it's two-character front headcode panel between the driving cab and the buffer beam. I would also see five Hull bound departures before my awaited 6.12pm steam train from York.

   But the 'piece de resistance' for me staying on at the station after school, would be the passing, not just of one but two lengthy goods trains from Bridlington, the first of which would have left the seaside town at 3.45pm. In 1960-1964, local wagon-load freight on the coast line was still very much buoyant. When I say lengthy, I mean long trundling goods trains of upto 70 wagons, comprising ventilator vans, open coal wagons and timber trucks too, long wheelbase pipe wagons and even the odd tanker truck and permanent way stock in the consist. It would have been a right medley of a freight train and not the uniform rakes you see today. These long freights would always have a Standard BR or ex-LMS style goods brake van on the rear, where the lonely guard would travel out his shift. But at least he had a pipe stove in there to keep him warm in winter! The awaited Gresley K3, LMS Ivatt or Standard Mogul (2-6-0's for those who don't know), or the ubiquitous WD or 'dub-dees' as we called them. Most of these locomotives would be Hull Dairycoates based (50B) and the long freight would terminate at Hull Priory Yard sorting sidings, heading due south at Cottingham South Junction on it's way. Priory Yard was the big marshalling yard in Hull where all freight trains were sorted for dispatch along the main line and incoming workings for the docks on the high level Hull & Barnsley line.

Sometimes, one of the station porters at Cottingham, would see to several wicker baskets that had been offloaded from a stopping train from the coast. They would contain ten to fifteen racing pigeons apiece and the porter would unstrap the flaps and all the birds would fly off en masse from many baskets, circle overhead and return home. I just loved watching that spectacle when it happened. Sadly, this novelty is long gone as the railways no longer bother with small time shipments.

I even got treat to the odd sighting of a weird unit rushing through towards Hull on those teatime spotting stopovers. I would always be alone at these times. I could see the gates close to traffic northwards at

MEMORIES OF COTTINGHAM STATION

Cottingham North. Then the southbound gates would close next at Thwaite Gates. Then the home starter signals would raise to the up position. I couldn't see any train approaching at first. Then a tiny blob would appear on the horizon, if I went up on the footbridge. It would get bigger and bigger as this thing approached the Hull-bound platform where I was spotting from. The station staff would never bother me, either. They could see I wasn't trouble on my own. This very low profile, four wheeled unit, black and with a yellow cab with chevrons of the same colours on front and back, would come wailing through the platform at high speed, blaring out a loud siren. The top of the cab would be no higher than platform level and this unit would have two or three men cramped inside. You've never seen anything so funny and odd in your life running on rails in between a very busy teatime train service. What I was looking at dashing through, was a Permanent Way self-propelled, Wickham trolley for track inspection gangs. This maybe only happened two or three times in those four years, but the event will always be there in my memory. The 5.45pm to Beverley was finally arriving and Dad would come over the footbridge to meet me....

As mentioned earlier, my father had walked out of the shipping office in Hull where he had been employed in the 1950s. In fact shipping agents, were the only employment Dad had known, all his working life until then, apart from being in the army during WWII. Very regrettably, he was to be out of work for two long years until 1962 when he found employment at Blackburn Engines aircraft factory, shortly to become Hawker Siddeley Aviation at Brough. This was a massive

DAVID KAY

change for him. I remember that first day of his at Brough, vividly. And after he left the 5.45pm to Beverley, I followed him and a new-found colleague all the way back up the snicket as they chatted together, right to entry onto New Village Road, when the other man went in another direction, before I was able to walk with my Dad alone for the remainder of the way home.

It would have been pretty nifty work in Brough, I expect. The factory claxons wouldn't ring out until 5pm. Coats on, and dash to Brough station, a mile away to board one of two lengthy workers trains put on for the thousands of factory workers in those days. I remember being on Hull Paragon platforms just once around that time. It was a dark winters night and I witnessed two twelve and thirteen coach trains arriving at two adjacent platforms with suburban stock within ten minutes of each other. One was steam hauled and would have stopped at Melton for Earle's Cement workers, Ferriby and Hessle, a Standard class 3 - probably 77002, the other, diesel hauled and come from Brough non stop a (Dairycoates, 50B allocated) class 37 diesel electric. Dad would have travelled with the other thousand plus passengers from all walks of the aircraft factory in the first of these trains. A lightning change of trains onto another platform (something you don't need to do today) and it would be the 5.38pm (24 hour clock hadn't been introduced yet), to Cottingham and Beverley formed of two, two-car Cravens units (class 105s for young readers). Dad would arrive on the platform at 5.45pm. I would greet him and announce that I was hanging around another half hour to see the 6.12pm from York. It was not to be missed as it would be steam

MEMORIES OF COTTINGHAM STATION

hauled until probably 1963.

Even by that year, steam power was beginning to die out in the Hull area and the 6.12pm from York was my favourite daily working, hauled by my beloved Thompson mixed traffic B1 or older Raven designed B16 engines of similar outline. Even to this day, the B1 is still one of my favourite engines and I'm glad to say that just two have been preserved out of the 410 built (61057 had been very badly damaged in 1950 in an accident, at just two years old and was then scrapped). As in the 10.2am from Bridlington, (described earlier), the 6.12pm would have vans attached either next to the loco's tender or on the tail (end of last passenger coach). Again, the consist would be a mixture of older Thompson and Gresley stock with maybe a couple of mark 1's thrown in for good measure. Occasionally, one of the vans could be a 'Blue Spot' fish van. Not for carrying fish but out of use for that traffic by then and used for parcels and small customers consignments of varying shapes and sizes. It would still house it's aluminium lining inside for its original use. The 6.12pm to Hull would return to York via Cottingham at 7.38pm that evening, but I regret that I never saw that train call at my local station, not even on the light, summer evenings.

Within the next couple of hours, during the short mid June to early September summer timetable operation on weekdays only, ran a non-stop returning Bridlington to Doncaster summer special which would pass Cottingham at about 7.35pm, having left Bridlington at 6.57pm and this was always a 36A Doncaster based B1 4-6-0 until diesels took over for the final few years this

DAVID KAY

Taken from Cottingham Station footbridge, a Class 40 diesel electric of the D2XX series slows for the stop on the 6.12pm from York. This was in the last two years of that line's existence, 1963-1965. Note the white discs showing 'Express Passenger Train'.

MEMORIES OF COTTINGHAM STATION

train was required. The morning outward run would have been at approximately 9.45am, having left Doncaster at 8.30am. It would in its last years of operation, have been a Brush diesel of type 2 or type 4 (class 31 or 47), depending on the load. Regretfully, once again, I never remember seeing this train pass either way, which was a great shame.

The lunchtime, 11.58am passing of the 3B01, mail and empty coaching stock parcels train from Hull Paragon's platform 12 (I did actually see it leave there once), to York, was another of my trainspotting highlights. A working timetable I got hold of recently, states that it stopped at Beverley, Market Weighton and Pocklington but Stamford Bridge and Earswick only when required. It was during the 1960s and headed by a York based Thompson B1 class steam locomotive (some with names) and was returning from the 9.33am (Cottingham departure time) York to Hull stopper. It would take all morning to take the engine off to the sheds at Dairycoates, turn it on the turntable, fill up the tender with water, top up the same with coal if necessary and get it back to Paragon Station a few miles away, for an 11.50am departure. The downside was, I mainly had to watch this train from the top-deck front window of an EYMS Beverley Bar-roofed bus, something also now extinct. (East Yorkshire Motor Services would put on a special school bus just as far as Hall Road for less than ten of us and it would always be a double decker and have a conductor too. But there strangely wasn't a returning service for the afternoons lessons). So as described earlier, I mainly saw this unique to Cottingham train, very briefly rip over the

Thompson B1 class No 61306 (now preserved) on the York line's last day, with snow on the ground.

The last day of services on the York line with a Cravens unit at Market Weighton.

MEMORIES OF COTTINGHAM STATION

gates, that had closed in front of my bus. It mainly comprised parcel vans and later, dedicated newspaper vans and some would be travelling empty to the then carriage works at York. I even remember on the odd occasion or two seeing the unusual sight of it having a DMU on the tail as if it was being 'top and tailed' as in today's parlance. But I did get treat in school holidays to seeing this train at very close quarters indeed, belting through the northbound platform at upto 60mph! It didn't half create a gush of wind as it passed the platform where I stood, disturbing any litter around into the air. I really enjoyed those brief seconds of pleasure.

In the last years of the York via Market Weighton line, the mail train as I called it, was handed over to a 2000hp Class 40 or 'whistler' diesel as they popularly became known at the time. This link between Beverley and York finally succumbed to the Beeching Axe on 27th.November 1965 and it was a fitting snowy winters day as I have photographs to prove it. The station staff actually had to shovel snow off the platforms on the very last day of service, being careful it didn't hit the railhead!

The 4.44pm 'Saturdays Only' from York really was the local trainspotter's treat of the week and ran in the summer months only. What was so special about this train then? It wasn't the usual Thompson B1 or Raven B16 that brought this train from York with carriage loads of disembarking train buffs, most of whom were much older than us. They were proper dedicated railway enthusiasts wielding cameras, just like I could be described, today. According to my 55 year old timetable, this service was daily, but only steam hauled

DAVID KAY

WD 2-8-0 class No.90352 hauls a local trip working J03 across the city.

MEMORIES OF COTTINGHAM STATION

on a Saturday. How strange. We were being treat to the sight and sound of a Stanier designed Jubilee Class 6P 4-6-0, another loco more akin to main line traffic. Perhaps it had been taken off a Liverpool to Newcastle express working at York, to haul a stopper to Hull via some of the lovely sounding stations at Earswick, Stamford Bridge, Pocklington, Londesborough, Market Weighton and Beverley. Kipling Cotes (famous for it's annual Derby horse race in March), between the latter two was only a request stop and was unmanned, even then. Not many trains called there. One particular remembered 'Jube' as we called them, was No.45581 *Bihar and Orissa,* (a state of India, but completely unheard of at our young age), was the loco in question on one particular Saturday afternoon. It was in its brunswick green express passenger livery and relatively speaking was usually a clean engine, I recall.

The station platform would be thronged with disembarked passengers, mainly of the male variety. Station staff would be collecting tickets at the barrier on Station Walk by the footbridge. I was down by the signal at the platform ends slope, talking to Gordon, my best trainspotting pal. 45581's driver opened the safety valves on the boiler top to relieve steam pressure. When this goes off, the sound of escaping steam at extremely high pressure makes an almost unbearable hiss. Its so loud, that you just cannot continue conversation even with the one standing beside you, but I just love the experience, being a steam fanatic. It went on for at least a minute, but seemed much longer. The 4.44 seemed to hang around for ages, possibly five minutes in dwell time. The platform cleared of people. The guard blew his whistle further down the train and *Bihar and Orissa* steams past me with its classic chuff, chuff, chuffing and gathering speed as it accelerates towards Thwaite Gates crossing. This was probably THE MOST fondly remembered event of my trainspotting days in the 1960s. Another Jubilee class engine that regularly worked this service, that comes to mind whilst browsing one of my many railway books, is No.45647 *Sturdee*. He was an admiral of the fleet during the late Victorian/Edwardian period. The 4.44pm from York was always a Jubilee class engine, or if it wasn't at least we did have an ex-LMS Stanier Black 5 instead, but not many of those carried nameplates. I probably just walked the mile to Cottingham Station to see this working, but it was certainly worth it!

The Stanier Jubilee engines, of which 191 were built, had been so named in honour of His Majesty King George V's Silver Jubilee in 1935 when they were new. The first was named *Silver Jubilee* and then the next 85 were named after British dependencies around the globe, followed by the rest after warships, admirals and mythological characters. No.45637 *Windward Islands* got written-off in a terrible, three train smash-up on a very foggy morning at Harrow & Wealdstone on the NW outskirts of London. It was piloting a Princess Pacific, the turbomotive No.46202 *Princess Anne* on a Liverpool bound express. It ran into the wreckage of two other trains that had already crashed. It was 8th.October 1952 when 112 were sadly killed and 340 others, injured. It was Britain's worst ever, peacetime rail disaster. Thankfully, there are still four Jubilees in main line operation today, either in lined brunswick

MEMORIES OF COTTINGHAM STATION

green or LMS crimson lake, which suited the class better.

I remember one year sometime in this glorious decade, Mum & Dad taking Jonathan my brother and I to Scarborough for the afternoon in a train composed entirely of compartment stock without toilets. We caught the 1.28pm **SX** (it left Cottingham ten minutes later on a Saturday). It was hauled by a Class 37 (English Electric Type 3 from 50B shed) and would have had at least nine carriages in the consist. But these suburban coaches were only 57 ft long as compared with the 63 ft of a corridor mark 1. Why we left our day trip to Scarborough so late, I know not. Anyway the 1.28pm called at every wayside station except Carnaby, Flamborough and Speeton. We had to 'cross our legs' until 3.1pm when our train pulled into Scarborough Central. I say Central Station, as Scarborough also had at the time another station called Londesborough Road to handle summer excursion traffic only. Scarborough station still has a long platform No.1 with the longest railway station seat on the network (or even the world), but such was the volume of summer extras, an additional station was needed to cope with demand! We would only have enjoyed just over four hours in the resort as my 1963/64 winter timetable shows the last train back leaving at 7.15pm and getting the Kay family back to Cottingham at 8.35pm by DMU. We then had a fifteen minute walk down 'the snicket' to reach our house.

An interloper on the North Eastern! An LMS Fowler tank backs its Hull-Beverley 'push pull' train out of the down platform. A sight the author well and truly missed.

MEMORIES OF COTTINGHAM STATION

CHAPTER 5
THE MORNING SHUNT

I would emerge from the kissing gate at the end of the snicket, cross the double tracks and find myself in a busy goods yard with an ageing 2-8-0 Austerity, ex-War Department (WD) class loco doing all the shunting work from Hull Dairycoates shed, coded 50B. The loco would date from 1943 when the Ministry of Supply employed outside contractors to build 732 of the type for immediate dispatch of many, to help in the war effort in Europe and the Middle East. The last, No.90732 had the name *Vulcan* on it's cabside, after the English Electric Vulcan works at Newton-le-Willows between Manchester and Liverpool where they were built. None were preserved, but the Worth Valley Railway did rescue an example from a clearing in a Swedish forest in 1973 and restore it to its former condition. I believe that it was dragged by rail from Hull Docks on the old high level, Hull & Barnsley line to Haworth yard and No.1931 was eventually renumbered 90733 in the series that ran from 90000. It's still one of my favourite engines in the Worth Valley preserved railway fleet as I now reminisce about these large engines doing the shunt in a small goods yard on a weekday & regrettably, school morning! I would have loved nothing more than to have stopped and watched

87

A typical platform ticket machine used by the author at Hull Paragon. This one is at a London Southern Region terminus.

MEMORIES OF COTTINGHAM STATION

to the bitter end and it's return to Hull.

The WD 8Fs eight coupled driving wheel flanges would squeal on the gentle curves of the track in the yard. There were coal trucks to sort. Full ones in for local domestic suppliers, who would arrive later in the morning in their lorries to pick up stock already bagged. And then there were the coal drops up an incline at the other side of the yard, past the then very new Danish Bacon Factory. This siding which would split into a double siding after the pedestrian crossing, was used by many pedestrians coming out of the snicket from New Village Road, or from Jesmond Road, Cornwall, Devon or Exeter Streets, joining the snicket along the way. Through the kissing gate and across the main running lines, past the goods shed doors and over the yard to climb a short slope and over the siding to continue into Cottingham, eventually coming out into Hallgate by the Junior Girls School, opposite St.Marys Church.

I do not recall seeing any such warning sign then present to show, **"Beware of Trains"**. Actually, they were only goods wagons being propelled very slowly by the locomotive at 3mph! In the opposite direction, coal wagons could be freewheeled with gravity down the incline. Younger readers won't know this, but in my day, loose-coupled goods wagons had the ability of being stopped manually, when a shunter could activate the brakes himself by releasing a long brake handle down each side. This could also be a treacherous job for the member of railway staff operating! But all the same, there was danger present to pedestrians during these shunting manoeuvres. Some would be 'hopper' trucks and would have bottom doors and their household coal

Top: Gresley 4-4-0 Hunt class No.62727 'The Quorn', named after a foxhunt in Leicestershire. On a parcels train, note the horsebox next to the loco.
Bottom: Thompson B1 class No.61084 rolls into Cottingham's 'up' platform with the 6.12pm stopping train from York on a wet evening.

MEMORIES OF COTTINGHAM STATION

loads would be emptied directly to the ground between the arches of the brick structure and then bagged up for household distribution.

Still at the west side of the yard, there were timber sawmills, were during the day, one could hear long planks of timber being sawn into usable sizes for customers orders. The timber would be brought in from Hull Victoria Dock which specialised in the import of timber only and then via Dairycoates Priory Yard sorting sidings in a propped up fashion by what was then known as 'wagonload' traffic. Cottingham used to receive European timber from the continent too. How do I know this? Because alongside the goods shed, where my friend Gordon and I dangled our feet to trainspot, there was sometimes a couple of what were known as continental ferry vans. I would never see these arrive or depart, though. (I have an example in my model railway collection and with sliding doors too). They would have come over on a Zeebrugge/Harwich train ferry. The morning shunt could take up to an hour, but alas, I could only stay a few minutes as I said earlier, I was destined for school and wouldn't want to be late. One of the station porters would be assisting there, coupling & uncoupling the wagon hooks with a long pole. The freight guard may have been helping as well. The loco crew remained on the footplate driving the engine at less than walking speed. It still had to be fired. There were still road vehicles dotted around the tarmac yard as well, with the rails set in, allowing room for wheel flanges. Cottingham goods yard could still be in the early 1960s, a dangerous place if care wasn't taken during this morning shunt.

DAVID KAY

When the shunt was finished, the consist would collect the brake van probably left down near the cattle ramp and then waited for a slot in passenger services to Hull and trundle back to Dairycoates sorting sidings near Hessle. Cottingham North crossing gates would still need to close to road traffic to allow the train to cross over to the 'up' line, before proceeding on it's way. This operation took part in Cottingham yard every weekday all year round, but it's still very vivid in my memory and fondly missed in todays modern railway operations. Wagonload freight on the Hull to Bridlington line finished for good in 1964 and the sidings then remained dormant for a further five years until British Rail decided it was time to rationalise the network and sell off any track and sleepers for scrap. As a steam aficionado, it was nice to know that steam remained king on goods traffic at Cottingham until the bitter end. 1964 was also the year I moved on at school and started attending the Secondary Modern, later to become Cottingham High.

MEMORIES OF COTTINGHAM STATION

CHAPTER 6
THE 25/- WEEKLY RUNABOUT TICKET

It was just coming up to the last week of July 1966 and we'd all just broken up from Cottingham Secondary modern school on Harland Way for the six week summer recess. I think there was just myself, Gordon, his brother Ramsay and possibly a tall lad called Adrian. We all had a meeting at Gordon's house in Lynngarth Avenue, off Beck Bank one afternoon after 'breaking up' as we called it and sat down at his dining table in the living room in front of the North Eastern Region timetable to discuss where we would go and what trains we would travel on the next week. Our meeting took no more than an hour or two and we skipped the tea & biscuits! This was Friday afternoon.

On the Monday morning we presented ourselves at Cottingham Station ticket office, not 200 yards from Gordon's house and handed over our twenty five shillings (or Bob, as the pre-decimalisation currency was nicknamed, - £1.25) to buy our N.E.Region weekly runabout tickets. This was probably the best ever value travel purchase of my entire life! We're probably looking at about £40-£50 or more, at today's prices. Fantastic value. Cottingham Station's booking office actually had a covered lean-to, probably of plywood and glass to keep passengers away from inclement

A Class 45/46 'Peak' diesel rushes a Summer Special to the Coast past the cattle ramp (behind the first coach) towards Cottingham North crossing.

It's 2019, and the author is still finding 'cops'. Seeing a locomotive for the first time ever!

Here, Britannia class Pacific, No.70000 "Britannia" in steam at a Charity Open Day at Crewe Diesel Depot in June.

MEMORIES OF COTTINGHAM STATION

weather as they purchased their tickets and made enquiries. We would be able to travel on any train within the North Eastern Region, although going up to the Newcastle area and the Tyne Valley line or even Middlesbrough, would have been excluded. West Yorkshire was our oyster! That week including Saturday, we travelled to every major town and city in that county including many minor ones too. We were not sightseers. We were on the hunt for train numbers to underline in our Ian Allan ABCs, with a particular emphasis to hunt down the dwindling number of steam locomotives which would by 1966, be mainly seen on freight, parcels and empty stock workings. We would be recording numbers of mainly, Stanier Black 5s, 8Fs and Robert Riddles' Standard designs, the latter not much more than ten years old, if that! (He was British Railways very last ever CME; Chief Mechanical Engineer). If we were really lucky, we may have 'copped' a 9F freight engine or two, that carried smoke deflectors at the front. Most of the trains we would travel on that week, were to be the ubiquitous multiple units, but there were also to be some nice treats along the way. I think we may even have spotted an early numbered 7P6F named, Britannia class loco (70000-70009), on a parcels at Leeds Whitehall Junction, but by this last year of its service, it was shoddy, unkempt and shorn of its nameplates. But we actually spotted a "Brit" from our DMU front window seat! Wow. I think that would have been 'The cop of the week'.

    Starting from Cottingham at 8.30am on that lovely summer's morning with the commuters going into town, we were treat to the pleasures of the comfort of a compartment on an inter-city express, albeit a DMU. It was none other than my favourite diesel unit of all time, the now extinct *Trans Pennine,* which had run up to Beverley on a warming up turn before getting ready for its three hour Hull-Liverpool service departing from Paragon at 9.10am. This six-car DMU even had a buffet car but not open for the short trip to Beverley. It was its stylish cab windscreens that made it so attractive to me. They curved round at the corners and in those days there were no complaining drivers seeing double signals, like what happened recently on the new class 385 electrics in Scotland!

    Later in the week, we would also have the pleasure of taking a seat on two loco-hauled expresses. One was a Newcastle-Liverpool train which had come off the main line at Northallerton and called at Ripon to arrive at Harrogate where we joined the Mersey-bound express. Ripon no longer has a station or even a train service and is probably one of the few cities in England without trains! (Ripon is a city as it has a cathedral!) That short-cut route was withdrawn under the Beeching Plan on 6th.March the following year.

    The second famous train we had the pleasure of riding was *The Devonian,* but regrettably only again, a short segment. This named train had started from Bradford Exchange and come to Leeds, possibly even with a steam tank engine which we didn't see. A 2500 horsepowered, Sulzer engined Peak diesel would back on, (reversal had been necessary at City Station, even though it had through platforms) and just take us as far as Sheffield Midland. But we always enjoyed sitting in compartments, knowing that this train was going all the

MEMORIES OF COTTINGHAM STATION

way to Kingswear on the South Devon coast!

The only time our small group left the environs of a railway station was to go and find another station in that city, usually on foot. Leeds main station was called *City* station, but until 1967, Leeds to London trains would leave from the platforms of another station called *Central,* just a short walk away.

Likewise, when we got to Sheffield Midland, we took the short walk over to Sheffield Victoria to see the 1500v.DC electric hauled trains of the Manchester, Sheffield & Wath railway hauled by ancient looking locomotives, some even designed before the war. The first EM1 Bo-Bo locomotive No.26000 *Tommy* had been built in 1941 and then put into storage because of hostilities. This new electrified main line wasn't inaugurated until as late as 1954, after the new Woodhead tunnel had been dug. Then, the longest tunnel in the kingdom at 4888 metres, (nearly five kilometres). Even Sheffield Victoria by 1966, was in a slow decline to death and would close ten years later to passenger trains.

We did not board any trains at Leeds Central or Sheffield Victoria, as at the latter, we had already run past the limit of our runabout tickets and strayed onto BR's Eastern Region with its dark blue running-in boards (station nameplates). North Eastern region's colour was a designated tangerine. Yet again, we just had to visit the two stations in the city of Wakefield. Westgate on the main line and Kirkgate for Leeds-Goole and local services to Pontefract, still with its three stations of Monkhill, Baghill and Tanshelf, albeit only small halts. Castleford and Huddersfield, but I cannot recall travelling from Wakefield Kirkgate towards Goole. This line is extremely moribund now, but still has three trains a day but only at rush-hour times for commuters.

Even today (April 2019), Sheffield Victoria station still exists because most of it sits on The Wicker viaduct which will never get demolished as it's probably a listed monument and the area is crowded with buildings and businesses and traffic. On a recent visit to Sheffield, I could see trees and foliage growing from the ballast where the tracks once laid on this main line across the Pennines.

Our runabout ticket area finished at the limits of the North Eastern Region. We had to pay a supplement to the guard/conductor to travel beyond Shipley and onto London Midland Region metals towards Keighley and Skipton. Their corporate colour was crimson. Strangely enough, the same was not required after Goole to travel through Thorne North (now my local station) and onto Doncaster and Mexborough. But for Sheffield we did. Their colours were dark blue. We enjoyed our weeks runabout ticket that much, that we did it all again the following year. On the 1967 excursions, we thought we'd get even more value out of our tickets and travel on the Sunday as well, as a starting off day. There were trains on the Hull-Scarborough line in those days on a Sunday, but only between mid-June and early September. No winter Sunday service, but thankfully there is today. By 1967, most of the green DMUs and maroon coaching stock had been repainted into British Rail's new corporate colours of plain blue for DMUs, (unless they were classified as express stock) and

MEMORIES OF COTTINGHAM STATION

blue/grey (off-white really), for loco hauled coaches and *The Trans Pennine*. British Rail was starting to look rather boring and bland and by August 1968 steam power would finish altogether. My interest in the then current rail scene was diminishing quite rapidly.

At one time, Normanton on the main line between Sheffield and Leeds was a very important junction station with a massive, sixty-foot wide island platform containing refreshment rooms from the days of the old Midland Railway, when early London to Glasgow express trains didn't have restaurant and buffet cars and the somewhat ten hour journey was interrupted halfway to Scotland, by a quick fifteen minute meal break, or buying items to take back on the train to consume later. Normanton looked the part. It indeed, had been in its day, a very important junction and changing point with full facilities and a platform canopy too. I really liked Normanton and it holds very fond memories. Today sadly, the platform still remains extant, but without the stately infrastructure. Just bus shelters protect passengers from inclement weather. And there's no longer long express trains calling, just a two-car class 158 DMU, even on a commuter, Leeds-Nottingham train when plenty of workers disembarked.

Me and my cadre of trainspotters never took part in a highly dangerous, possibly dirty and illegal practice of what trainspotters called 'Shed Bashing'. I do have underlinings in my Ian Allan ABC combined volume that Hull Dairycoates, Leeds Holbeck and even York sheds had been 'bashed', but in reality, we had just viewed them and their steam and/or diesel powered contents from a distance. With one exception. I remember, we had quite a wait for our next train back from Normanton, so we decided to go and 'bash the shed' at what was coded 55E in the North Eastern Region's Leeds division. We could see the tantalising, grimy looking motive power looming out of the simple two-road straight shed, just to the north of the platform. We surely must have trespassed over the tracks to access Normanton MPD. I don't remember seeing the shed foreman about. Normanton was a small shed by most steam shed standards....very small. But there would also have been engines in the shed yard.

What we spotted that day would have been Crabs, LMS mogul 2-6-0s, Stanier Black 5 and 8Fs and possibly a WD 2-8-0 and as a special treat, a 9F without blinkers called a Crosti-boiler, because of its unique design. Possibly No.92025, but I'm not sure. Only ten were built. A large freight engine with ten coupled wheels (2-10-0) and no smoke deflectors, that could haul the heaviest trains on the main line down to Cricklewood in London with Yorkshire coal. We squeezed down the dirty brick walls between the engines, still warm from their last duties. I seem to remember nobody about at all. If Adrian had been with us in 1966, he'd even have been suited & booted. That was Adrian Boynton. You couldn't go round an engine shed without getting dirty. It was impossible. But we certainly did 'shed bash' 55E Normanton that day in July. And that was the only ever time in my life, I did it properly. It was highly illegal and dangerous and one really had to apply in advance to railway offices in order to get a shed permit, but none of us trainspotters ever bothered and usually the foreman turned a 'blind eye',

The author's favourite steam locomotive of all time. The preserved Stanier Coronation Pacific No.6229 "Duchess of Hamilton" was finally streamlined in 2009 at the NRM, York after much debate. I love it. Its the epitome of engine design but sadly it will never steam again.

This is Hull Corporation Pier Railway Station today, the only location in Britain that never had a train. You parked your car, and went into the building to buy your tickets for the Humber Ferry to New Holland, before the bridge was opened in 1981.

The author's "Wildebeeste" wooden nameplate bought for £55 which sadly didn't survive ten years. The real cast one looking the same, would have been £10,000 at auction. Two should exist somewhere!

I bought this at a railwayana auction in 2017. It wasn't cheap and wasn't in this livery at the time. I have repainted it in North Eastern Region 'tangerine', which was the colour I was familiar with, in my day as a trainspotter. It's a seat back plate from the Hull to Selby line and Wressle is still open today. It's my home nameplate.

Top left: A permanent reminder that Hull was 'UK City of Culture' in 2017, on the side of a Class 180 Adelante unit, soon to be replaced on Hull Trains' Hull & Beverley to London runs.

Top right:
Potted ferns and flowers advertising Hull Trains sit on the platform at Hull Paragon, something unheard of in my day as a trainspotter!

Right:
A Jubbly frozen ice drink which is still available today, I'm told.

An unliveried bi-mode, Class 802 'Azuma' unit in Hull Paragon on a demonstration, press launch run to the city. These trains now perform the daily LNER "Hull Executive" service to Kings Cross.

An LNER 'Azuma' unit at Doncaster's Platform 1 in full livery, heads out on a Leeds to Kings Cross working.

MEMORIES OF COTTINGHAM STATION

anyway! So that was what 'Shed Bashing' was all about.

Our last treat would be an educational school trip in 1969 with many other schools from the East Riding down to London to visit the Science, Victoria & Albert and British Museums. Obviously, the opportunity was taken to trainspot along the way from the carriage window of this special charter service. In 1970, I left school and started work. The opportunity arose for me to actually sell and despatch those famous *Edmondson* card railway tickets so well known throughout railway history, at Thomas Cooks, as I was put in charge of that department and even doing the monthly book-keeping. I decided it was time to pack up my notebook and Ian Allan ABCs for underlining numbers in, and just become a non-spotting railway enthusiast. My glory days of the golden 60s were over!

One day on our travels, we really pushed the boat out big style and left the station at Victoria/Exchange in Manchester (these two stations were joined together by then, the longest platform in the country at 682 metres!) and caught a bus to Piccadilly and we actually boarded an electric-hauled express to Crewe! The Mecca of all trainspotting locations. Wow, that was an exciting day, even passing the famous Jodrell Bank telescope along the way, but you had to be quick to see it near Sandbach as our train sped past at 100mph! I know that day would have been completely divorced from our weekly runabout tickets, but I just had to mention Crewe. I remember a lady on the bus in Manchester city centre asking us if we were half fare. To me, it sounded like: 'Are you off there?', in her Mancunian accent. What was it of any business of hers, anyway? The bus wasn't full,

Top: A D49 'Hunt class' loco No.62765 'The Goathland' passing the cattle ramp over Cottingham North crossing with a stopping train for Hull, around 1957.

Bottom: A Thompson Mixed Traffic B1 class loco storms out of Bradford Exchange with another portion of the Yorkshire Pullman. Note the mixture of liveries, so this would be a 1967 view.

MEMORIES OF COTTINGHAM STATION

(when we should have been giving up our seats to our elders!)

On our train out of Hull on the main line to the west, after Hessle Road flyover, it passed a storage yard at Dairycoates known as Seven Section Sidings. This location was the penultimate stopping-off point for redundant and withdrawn steam locomotives on their way to their very sad end under the cutters torch in the yards of the famous Hull scrapman, Albert Draper & Sons. The Locomotives in question, possibly minus a few fittings including nameplates where applicable, would have been brought to these sidings near Dairycoates shed by a diesel locomotive hauling possibly upto half a dozen at a time from their depots all around Yorkshire and even possibly further afield, too. The masses of sidings were located on the sweeping curve adjacent to the running lines between Hessle Road flyover and the girder bridge running over a single siding that now serves a cement works. This was 1964-1967. The engines final journey, would again be with the power of another diesel loco to the nearby Neptune Street yard, or Drapers main site off Bankside Sculcoates, now known as **HU5.**

I remember getting into the unlocked yard there one Sunday afternoon by bike in 1969, or maybe climbing over a wall and climbing aboard the single cabs of D2701 and its sister D2702, 0-4-0 diesel hydraulic shunters, that had even been withdrawn by this date. Yes, I know I was trespassing! As will be detailed later in chapter 8, hydraulic power wasn't standard and had only been favoured by the Western Region. They had both been built by the North British Loco Works in

103

DAVID KAY

Two class 158 units in the platforms of Cottingham at the same time (photo taken from the bridge)

MEMORIES OF COTTINGHAM STATION

Glasgow, the same year I was born and had done their time shunting and found themselves in locations where no more work was available.

Seven Section Sidings at Hull Dairycoates was just a smattering compared to where many redundant steam locomotives would be towed to, to end their lives. Seven Section would accommodate possibly two dozen engines at a time. All Southern and Western Region examples, along with many from the London Midland, would finish their days in a massive yard on Barry Docks in South Wales. It was run by a Welshman called Dai Woodham and his family business. He started receiving steam hulks in 1964, but it was more profitable and much quicker to scrap wagons instead. Locos took five days to dismember. The locomotives started to accumulate, as steam sheds within 200 miles of there, closed. By 1968 when steam finished altogether, our little group, or even just Gordon & I should have gone down to Barry. I believe Gordon did get there, but not me. But it was a hell of a trek and the return journey would never have been accomplished during daylight hours, even in mid Summer. My parents would never ever have allowed me at even fifteen, to stay out overnight, B&B or not! And another thing, pocket money just didn't run to a mega trip like this. It was a 250 mile journey each way. And borrowing from the bank of Mum & Dad was just unthinkable. So, I had to forget this one and let it slide away.

Dai Woodham and his team did cut some locos up but not many. Over the years he accumulated 213 specimens from all over, but as expected only one from the Eastern Region: It just had to be one of my

105

favourites, the now preserved Thompson B1 class No.61264, that had finished its working career as a stationary boiler at Colwick shed, Nottingham. All these specimens were rescued by preservationists, thankfully.

In 1980, I moved to Bristol with work, for a couple of years. Steam had finished twelve years earlier. It would have been just an hours drive to Barry scrapyard in my trusty Vauxhall Viva over the Severn Bridge. I didn't really have time for reading, not even the railway press. Something else I now very much regret. I missed out on 25 years of up to date railway news. I thought driving to Barry would have been a complete waste of time and money with the yards completely empty by then. I didn't find out until 1989 when I bought a book about the 'preservation miracle' there, that back in 1980, there were still 95 rusting hulks exposed to the salty air of the Bristol Channel. They all got rescued, the last one not leaving until 1990. I was literally gutted and couldn't turn the clock back nine years. I only wish I could have!

Back at Seven Section Sidings. There were always two rows of steam locomotives awaiting their fate on lines right next to the main running line. We would be on our train heading for Doncaster or somewhere else and it had just passed under the new flyover on Hessle Road. Books and pens at the ready. We would have to scribble down right fast as many of these redundant hulks numbers as we could as our train sped past quite quickly. Naturally, we would not see anything of the engines in the row behind. After the rush past, we would then confer between ourselves and find we had only missed one or two individuals. This was the art of

MEMORIES OF COTTINGHAM STATION

trainspotting and we loved the adrenalin rush. All types of ex-LMS & ex-LNER engines and even ten year old standard types were brought to Seven Section on a regular basis in the 1960s. These ranged from 8F & local WD engines to even a good selection of Gresley named A3 and A1 ECML classes. Even a Stanier Jubilee talked about earlier, No.45581 *Bihar & Orissa* is recorded as being cut-up by Albert Draper's team on 19th.December 1966.

A group of individuals tried desperately to save the very last Peppercorn A1 Pacific from Draper's oxyacetylene torches; No.60145 *Saint Mungo* in the summer of 1966, but couldn't raise the required finance in time, so lost the opportunity to save the last one for posterity. Hence the setting up of the *A1 Steam Locomotive Trust* twenty-four years later to build from scratch, a brand-new Peppercorn Pacific which **we** have called *Tornado* and numbered it 60163 to continue the sequence, but this is another story and can be found elsewhere. I say **WE,** as I am a covenantor of this organisation who are very proud of their achievements, but it did take eighteen years for *Tornado* to become a reality! There were critics who said it couldn't be done, but we proved them wrong. The A1 Trust are now well on with their second project *Prince of Wales* No.2007, a Gresley P2 and it's expected to steam in 2021 or 22. Albert Draper himself saved a Stanier Black Five, No.45305 as this was the cleanest example in his yard and this locomotive eventually got named *Alderman A.E.Draper* (himself), and this can still be seen running today in its preserved condition on heritage lines and the main line too.

Oh, Yes... Hull's own B1, No 61010, 'WILDEBEESTE' Photographed at Bridlington in 1963

The four-character headcode panel on a Trans Pennine DMU at Selby. 2 showed signalmen that the train was a stopping passenger service, L showed its travelling to Leeds in this area and 99 was the route number. This facility became obsolete with the introduction of TOPS in 1973.

MEMORIES OF COTTINGHAM STATION

The Thompson designed B1 Class of mixed traffic locomotives were introduced from 1942 to 1949 and eventually 410 examples were outshopped from various works, numbered 61000 to 61409. The first forty-one examples except one: 61036 *Ralph Assheton* were all named after antelopes, deer and ibex like breeds of goat. Later, this class were named after LNER executives and Lords and one 61379, was named *Mayflower* after the boat the Pilgrim Fathers sailed to the New World in. I'm pleased to say that this name lives on, being carried by 61306, that took us to Withernsea in 1963 (see later). Why am I rambling on about the Thompson B1 mixed traffic class so much? This was my very favourite class, containing my very favourite Hull-based locomotive: No.61010 *Wildebeeste.* We would spot *Wildebeeste* on a very regular basis hauling all types of train as this individual would be based at Hull sheds all it's short life from 1947 to 1966. It started out being allocated to 53B Hull Botanic Gardens, before transferring to 53A when 53B/50C became dieselised, later to become 50B Hull Dairycoates. *Wildebeeste* would finally succumb to Albert Drapers team's oxyacetylene torches on 28th.February 1966, just nineteen years old. It had operated to and from Hull all this time. I was that besotted with this engine's name, that in 2008/9 I had a wooden replica nameplate made for me by a gentleman who used to advertise in the pages of *Moorsline,* the quarterly periodical of the North Yorkshire Moors Railway. He lived in a village near Lincoln and had it despatched to me for £55 including postage. Sadly, he no longer does this work. If I'd gone to a railwayana auction and bid for the real one of two only, actually off engine No.61010, it would have set me back around £10,000. Ten Thousand Pounds! Sadly, my cheap nameplate too, has now also been scrapped. It was made of softwood and not really designed for outdoor use on my home and got severely warped as it faced south in the sun!

I did go later to a railwayana auction and won my bid for a station seatback plate in LNER colours of apple green and cream, from a Hull to Selby line station still open for traffic today (Wressle) and this I could well afford. This is cast iron and will outlive my home! It's already nearly a hundred years old and looks brand new. I did actually repaint my cherished Wressle seatback plate in North Eastern Region tangerine, as this book was being finalised. Please see colour plates after Page 100.

MEMORIES OF COTTINGHAM STATION

CHAPTER 7
STEAM BOWS OUT AT COTTINGHAM

It was Saturday 2nd.September 1967 and I had been trainspotting on that summer morning, as usual. It would be the last day of summer operation of the season when the timetable would revert to winter service operation from the following day, but with no trains on a Sunday, then on this line. This was the case until a much later date. At around 10.50am every summer Saturday until that year, us trainspotters had the pleasure of witnessing the passing of the last remaining steam-hauled summer special. It was from Bradford Exchange picking up at Leeds City along the way, destined for Bridlington and had left Bradford at 0820, along with another steam hauled 0820 to Poole in Dorset, both powering their trains along, side by side! By, that must have been a fantastic spectacle to the observer. The former carried the reporting number *1H92* on a special wooden board slotted onto the top smokebox door lamp iron. The loco that day was a Stanier Black 5, No.44662 from Low Moor Shed at Bradford, coded 56F in the Wakefield division. The shed would close later that year when all steam power was eradicated from the North Eastern Region and the enthusiast would have to travel to Lancashire depots to find the last lingering steam traction. At the time, we

DAVID KAY

The 1H92 with Patricroft based (Salford), Standard class 5MT, No.73141, a Caprotti valve geared engine.

MEMORIES OF COTTINGHAM STATION

were reduced to spotting from our tiny outpost on the hilly mound beside the billboard at Thwaite Gates crossing. It would pass us at a steady speed, trailing nine or ten standard mark 1 maroon coaches with possibly the odd one or two BR new blue/grey liveries included in the consist.

I had my bicycle with me this day, as I'd been invited for lunch to my mother's family at Sutton Road, just short of three miles away. My great aunt Mary was there too, but I couldn't linger. I had to get back for the afternoon's passing of the very last, steam-hauled summer special, still carrying the *1H92* reporting number, although strictly speaking, it should have been coded *1L92* as the Bridlington-Bradford train was heading back to the Leeds area and into the history books! I was back on the 'down' platform in plenty of time to see the passing of *1H92* and to lament as the last coach passed me showing its corridor vestibule connection and over Thwaite Gates, round the bend towards Snuff Mill Lane and into the distance and out of sight for ever. This was the best location to watch its passing as I could then view the motion, which wouldn't be cut-off by the platform. I was clever, even at fifteen years old! There was a man stood next to me taking a sound recording and in those days tape-recorders were extremely heavy and bulky. As mentioned earlier, the morning shunt had terminated three years before in 1964, and this sighting was the very last, non-preserved steam locomotive to pass through Cottingham Station under British Railways ownership on a regular working. I had witnessed history at 2.12pm that September afternoon and wouldn't have missed it for the world!

DAVID KAY

My best and closest trainspotting pal Gordon, wasn't there on that historic afternoon. I believe he could have been away in Scotland on his family's annual pilgrimage to Greenock to visit family for their holidays, when they also went over to the Isle of Arran to pursue some special activity of which I knew not at the time. I remember him telling me that one year in 1963, returning from Scotland he had seen a purple A4 Gresley Pacific (60029, *Woodcock*) in York station on 5th.September. It was actually a shade of blue that looked purple under certain lighting conditions.

That was the day my Mum and aunt Norah took Jonathan and I to the Castle Museum and old Railway Museum at York. The latter was just a glorified shed and not the wonderful, G.T.Andrews building we see today. It was housed in the old railway terminus in Queen Street which closed in 1877 when York's present trainshed opened. The original pre-1877 building still exists and now houses a car rental depot. We asked to linger a while to trainspot when we got there. I'm glad we did. We would witness the passing of a Southern Region based Class 33, Sulzer diesel heading south with a long train of cement empties through the then centre roads, the diesel a rarity on the North Eastern Region. This was the only time I travelled on the York via Market Weighton line. We travelled out by DMU and returned on the 5.8pm, loco-hauled class 40 service getting us back to Cottingham at 6.12pm as described elsewhere. Dad had beaten us that day on his return from work at Brough aircraft factory on the 5.45pm Beverley train and would therefore have to wait a long time for his tea!

MEMORIES OF COTTINGHAM STATION

Steam in the Hull area had finished by 1967 and Dairycoates shed had been turned over to diesel only. Very sadly, wagonload traffic on the railways declined and declined as trends became modernised with containerisation and bulk flows of today, until in 1969 there was no longer any need to send a locomotive to shunt goods yards up and down the nation where nearly every station on the network had a goods yard. Can you believe it? Cottingham's morning shunt was no longer needed after 1964. This was the year I started attending the Secondary Modern school at Harland Way and I would only pass over Cottingham North crossing gates by bicycle riding in-tandem with my friend Adrian. So looking to our left would not have resulted in seeing any distant puffs of white smoke in the goods yard, regrettably! It would have been one of the ill-fated class 14, Swindon built 0-6-0 diesel hydraulic shunters of which Dairycoates shed had 33 allocated, if shunting had continued for just those five more years. I don't ever recall even seeing a Dairycoates based Class 37 diesel doing the honours in place of a failed WD. It may on one or two occasions have been an Ivatt LMS Mogul (No's 43XXX), deputising. Steam engines were actually more reliable than diesel motive power and cheaper to build, but so old fashioned and extremely labour intensive. The morning shunt was withdrawn in 1964 then, Cottingham yard stood empty and void of movement and the siding lines were eventually ripped up and rationalised and today you have to travel long distances by train to see any signs of what we would call goods yards or freight sidings in modern parlance. Such is progress.

DAVID KAY

CHAPTER 8
HULL & BARNSLEY TRACKS

I feel this book wouldn't be complete without describing two other fabulous trainspotting locations, but still on the Cottingham line and within four miles of there. It was now the 1966 to 1968 era and I would cycle for fifteen minutes to a little concrete footbridge over the double tracks by the Ideal Standard/Stelrad works and the bridge would overlook their sports ground where I could sometimes view tennis matches in progress, even though I didn't know the game. This location was known as Waterworks Crossing. Michael Marsden mentions this location in his railway dvd of Hull, *Marsden Rail No.12*.

It was a spring or summer's afternoon. The footbridge would link National Avenue and Woodgate Lane, linking one to connect with Brooklands Road, off Spring Bank West, where I would later buy a house just over ten years in the future. What was so special about coming here to trainspot for a couple of hours? The footbridge overlooked another overbridge carrying purely freight traffic on the remnants of the Hull & Barnsley Railway's all, high-level line across the city of Hull from the docks in the east to the sorting sidings in the west. In 1966 and the following year, one of my old favourites, the WD 2-8-0s were still very much the

MEMORIES OF COTTINGHAM STATION

mainstay of local trip workings in Hull and upto forty were still allocated to 50B shed, Dairycoates. It was just great to be able to witness long trundling freight trains on another route. Again, there would be a variety of types of load carried, all to and from the docks for export and import from anywhere in the world. I wasn't really bothered very much about the DMUs whizzing under me on their way to Cottingham or Hull. Beyond the overbridge, I could just make out Walton Street crossing and the junction laid in 1924 by the LNER to connect the two lines. This would be when Hull & Barnsley trains finished running to Cannon Street Station, which had been rather inaccessible for passengers and the new company wanted all Cudworth (never Barnsley) traffic, to run into Hull Paragon. I must mention that there had also once been a shed/stabling point for shunting engines on Alexandra Dock and also coded 50B as a sub-shed of Hull Dairycoates until the early 1960s. The allocated shunting only engines mainly had to stable outdoors as the structure was in terrible disrepair. The number of WDs started dwindling as British Rail's North Eastern Region started running down steam in 1966, to be eliminated completely the following year. These powerful engines built for the war effort, were sadly replaced with something rather pathetic.

BR's Western Region was focussed on diesel hydraulic motive power, rather than diesel electric as was the rest of the country. Diesel hydraulic powered engines were never successful or more reliable than diesel electric. In 1964, Swindon Works built 56 Paxman 0-6-0 shunting and trip working locomotives

117

with Ventura engines and hydraulic transmission. They were useless and prone to unreliablity, but yet thirty-three got shipped to Hull Dairycoates shed in 1966 to replace the dwindling number of WDs. The Paxman Ventura's (classed 14 under TOPS computerised system BR launched in 1973) were just of 650 brake horsepower which meant that double-heading was necessary on most freights. This included trip workings I saw on the high level line across the city. They performed the mainstay of this traffic after steam had been finished in the Hull area, until they too were sadly withdrawn due to breakdowns even before the 1970s arrived. I enjoyed my trips to Waterworks Crossing but better still, I really savoured my mornings on Hull's Paragon Station, a little further down the line....

MEMORIES OF COTTINGHAM STATION

CHAPTER 9
HULL PARAGON, MY MECCA OF TRAINS

It was 1963, I seem to recall and I was ten years old. My parents finally entrusted me to catch a bus into Hull, buy a platform ticket which was then a penny (1d), which during my visits went up to 2d. and get the bus home without getting into trouble. So it was and I caught the Hull Corporation double-decker bus No.15 service from the Inglemire Lane stop on Hall Road. They still, well and truly had conductors in those days until 1971. I can't remember what the child fare was but I do know I had change from one shilling (1/-, now 5p), after getting two buses and a platform ticket. I bought nothing else as I didn't eat sweets like normal kids did and only had a quarter of Holland toffees from the top shop (as we called it) round the corner on Inglemire Lane, now and again! The platform ticket was duly purchased from one of two red vending machines available near the platform barriers. I would show it to the ticket collector. It was really only available for just an hour for folk to see their friends and relatives off on trains, but I would really outstay my welcome and stay on those sacred platforms at Paragon Station for two-and-a-half hours!

I was allowed through onto Platform 8. To my left were the pristine cars (never carriages or coaches, note!)

of *The Yorkshire Pullman*. Four burnt umber and cream Pullman cars with majestic names after birds or precious stones. These were the first class, one palour (saloon car) and one being a kitchen car, but with seating too. All passengers on the *Yorkshire Pullman* were served meals and drinks at their seats. Then there would be a second class car, also kitchen or palour cars with schedule numbers from Car No.311 to Car No.354, called *Hadrian Bar* but this last one does not come within the remit of this book. These cars had been built by Metropolitan-Cammell in Birmingham in 1960 and were based on the standard mark 1 bodyshell of 1951, but these Pullmans were still only three years old. Next in the 10.10am London Kings Cross train's consist was a completely different Pullman style of car and was of the old, straight sided design from the same company and built by the Metropolitan Carriage & Wagon Company and dating from way back in 1928, but refurbished since. These were numbered Car No.62 to Car No.80 with gaps in Pullman's schedule. These would also be second class and would contain the brake van with storage space for passengers luggage. People, especially the well-to-do and wealthy did not travel lightly in those days and would have already taken their seats by the time I strolled the platform towards the engine, taking in the sumptuousness of my surroundings.

 The luxurious Pullman trains always had attendants standing by each door and kitted out in crisp white jackets with blue lapels and cuffs, finished off with brass buttons and Pullman badges to greet passengers onto the train and direct them to their seats. They wore

MEMORIES OF COTTINGHAM STATION

navy blue waistcoats underneath and their trousers had a light blue stripe down the leg. This was still the age of luxury train travel. Pullman passengers where treat like royalty and I was there, a ten-year old trainspotter on Platform 8 awaiting *The Yorkshire Pullman's* imminent departure. Next and last in line before the engine was a full brake carriage known to us trainspotters as a **BG** van and in the traditional standard maroon livery. It would be in Pullman burnt umber and cream if it was running today in a charter service.

Other portions from Harrogate and after 1948 Bradford, all joined together at Doncaster. In 1961 or 1962, this short Pullman train connecting with the main train at Doncaster, from Harrogate and Bradford/Leeds formed a lengthy thirteen coach consist, was no longer a Dairycoates based B1, D49, K3 or even a V3 steam tank engine for this light load. This is what hurts and always will. I was born too late and missed what I really would have liked to have seen those mornings I came to witness the Pullman's departure to the capital. The steam engine had been replaced with a class 40 Diesel of the D200 or D300 series by 1963, the latter showing its four-character headcode panel, (train reporting number to signalmen along the line). The D200s had a plain nose end with yellow 'cheesebox' but originally carrying white fold-up reporting discs, instead. We called these engines English Electric Type 4s. They were also known to us trainspotters as 'whistlers' as that was the noise they made when idling in stations. 10.10am duly arrived and *Yorkshire Pullman* slowly slid away from Platform 8 to arrive in Kings Cross at 2.3pm with lunch served at passengers seats. More on the

What the author just missed: V3 tank No.67640 stands at Hull Paragon Station's Platform 8 with the Hull portion of the Yorkshire Pullman. No later than 1962.

A Metropolitan Cammell Mark 1 Pullman car used on North Eastern Region services including the Yorkshire Pullman. All first class cars were named after ladies or precious stones. This is a second class car.

MEMORIES OF COTTINGHAM STATION

Pullmans, later.

The Hull and Selby Railway arrived in the city in 1846 with the opening of a station in Railway Street. This was never going to prove big enough for future demand and also it was not centrally located down the west side of Humber Dock, now the marina. The site is now occupied by a boat yard. The architect G.T.Andrews, who built most of the railway stations on the Hull-Scarborough line designed and built Paragon Station as we still know it today. It was opened on 8th.May 1848 with the adjoining Royal Station Hotel, also designed by Andrews, for The York & North Midland Railway.

Hull's luxury Pullman train had left for London and I spent another two hours wandering its ten public platforms, although when built was provided with fourteen which it still had in 1963. I would like to give you a brief tour as I wandered about watching with interest the arrivals and departures throughout the remainder of those mornings. Lets remember then, that Paragon Station tracks come in from the west. Over to the north side, we start with platforms 1 & 2, used solely by the Hornsea and Withernsea trains. These would be empty after 19th.October 1964 when the two branches would be withdrawn by our friend, Doctor Beeching. They shared a track as far as Wilmington, where the tracks went their seperate ways. I didn't bother with them much as most services were handled by class 105 Cravens of Sheffield, DMUs operating in twin-car sets coupled together to form longer trains when demand permitted. Platforms 3 to 8 would handle the general medley of trains to and from the Coast Line,

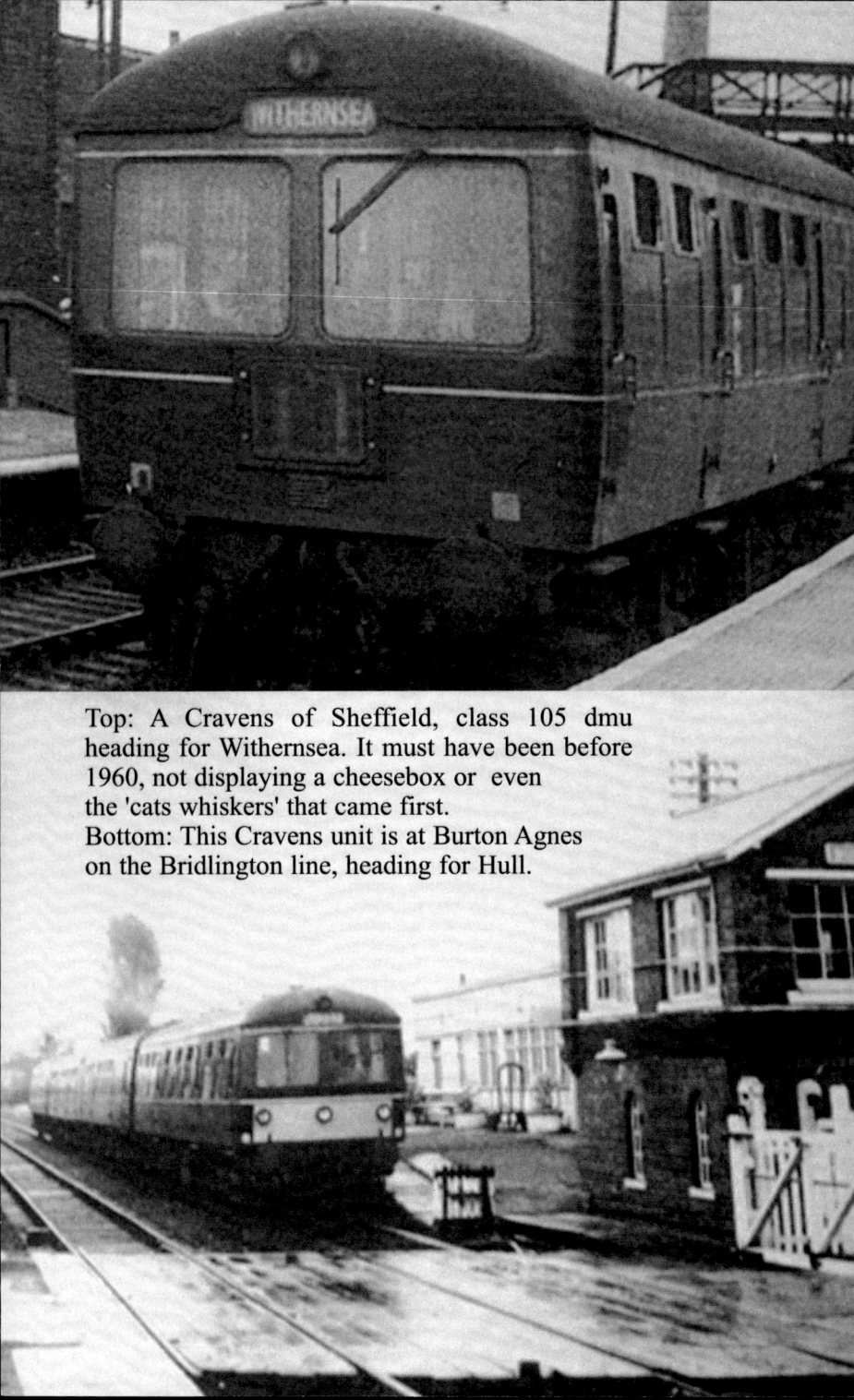

Top: A Cravens of Sheffield, class 105 dmu heading for Withernsea. It must have been before 1960, not displaying a cheesebox or even the 'cats whiskers' that came first.
Bottom: This Cravens unit is at Burton Agnes on the Bridlington line, heading for Hull.

MEMORIES OF COTTINGHAM STATION

York, Leeds, Brough, Selby, Goole, Doncaster, Sheffield, *The Trans Pennine* DMU and of course the few London trains as there were then, not the number there are today. *Yorkshire Pullman* was usually the only one I normally saw, unless I called on occasion at other times of the day. Manchester as a destination in the 1960s was rare, whereas today all *Trans Pennine Express* Class 185 DMUs terminate at Manchester Piccadilly. You cannot get a through train to Manchester Airport or even Liverpool Lime Street. How bizarre in this day and age!

Platform 9 was not serving a passenger service at that time. (Todays Platform 2 and used mainly for *First Hull Trains* services to London). It was always filled all morning long by a long rake of parcels & empty newspaper vans and stretched at least as far as the trainshed roof. This stock would be joined by a couple of passenger carriages during the early evening to form the then, last train of the day to Doncaster leaving at 9.27pm. Upon reaching Doncaster, the parcels stock would then be detached and moved to another platform by their station pilot and joined to another overnight train reaching London Kings Cross at 2.56am or even distributed to other cities with parcels for the Royal Mail. I once saw this train pulling out of Platform 9 from Park Street overbridge railings with a Class 47, (Brush type 4) at the head on a summer evening when it was still light. I was on a bike ride.

Just to the left of Platform 9, was a tiny little platform 10, only capable of handling a two-car DMU but was never used as such. It was built for fish and fruit traffic. Platform 10 was therefore always empty in the

DAVID KAY

1960s during my visits and as Platform 1 now, still is. I don't think I've ever seen this bay being used!

Still looking over to one's left on the south side were Platforms 11-14, the last two stretching from the parcels office half way down the building, right as far as Park Street overbridge and then the other side of here, Paragon Station power signalbox, still in use today, but probably not for much longer when York's Rail Operating Centre (ROC) will take over in future years.

Platforms 13 & 14 had been built without canopies for the once, short-lived emigrant trade, when northern Europeans and those from the Baltic states where passing through Northern England to seek new lives in America. They had disembarked from ships arriving at Hull Docks and would continue their journeys by rail to Liverpool from where the steamers set sail across the Atlantic. Latterly, these platforms had been used for the lengthy Saturday afternoon specials to Boothferry Park's football ground platform for Hull City AFC home matches. There could be up to ten such trains each way depending on who *City* were playing as outward and return departure times were always advertised in *Hull Daily Mail* on a Friday evening. I sadly, never went down to Paragon Station on a Saturday afternoon to witness this spectacle, something I do regret. Today the platforms stand isolated and unloved and totally unused and weedstrewn.

Platforms 11 & 12 were the parcels platforms, from where the 11.50am '3B01' mail train to York left from, until 1965 when the section from Beverley closed, described earlier. Today, they stable the *Hull Trains* empty stock overnight, off the Kings Cross-Beverley

MEMORIES OF COTTINGHAM STATION

service as there is no facility whatsoever of holding the five-car Class 180 Adelante unit at the latter, as described earlier. All station sidings and yards were rationalised in 1970 and taken out. As mentioned in the Hull & Barnsley section, when I lived off Spring Bank West in the late 1970s, I once saw a former *Trans Pennine* DMU shuttling to Boothferry Park's single platform, coming off Spring Bank West's overbridge and behind the petrol station there on the embankment. By this time, its griddle buffet car had long since been removed due to lack of patronage. The football specials shortly finished thereafter, as spectators started driving to football matches rather than using special train or bus services laid on for them.

Over to the north side of Paragon Station were masses of storage sidings. These would be quite full of spare coaching stock most of the year and were used solely for summer extras to the coast. In addition to this, there was also a carriage depot down the far side of Hull fairground on Walton Street. I remember seeing plenty of stock stabled there, mainly older Thompson-designed carriages in maybe 1962, when someone took me in their car down Walton Street the evening before the summer special excursion season would commence in mid-June. These carriages were very distinct in that they were fitted with white oval toilet windows, also sometimes in the centre rather than at vestibule ends. I was with another Adrian childhood friend and his Dad (driving the car), who lived in our street and owned a good model railway layout I was envious of. His Dad was taking us to his Woolworth shop on Anlaby Road where he managed at the time. He must have left something at his office and wanted to retrieve it. This was a special treat. Its amazing what one can still remember nearly sixty years on!

There were also coal drops amongst these sidings as steam locomotives were still using Hull Paragon on occasion. The station was such a busy terminus in the early 1960s that not one but two 0-6-0 diesel mechanical shunting engines of 204bhp would be stationed all the time at the outer end of the platforms, one on the north side, one on the south side. D2169 and D2170 look familiar numbers underlined in red in my 1968 Ian Allan British Rail Locomotives and other Motive Power combined volume purchased for 12/6 in that year. I still have this edition, but I'm upset that older copies got destroyed, once underlined numbers had been transferred with my brother Jonathan's assistance. Once again, I had missed a steam loco acting as station pilot at Paragon and even in 1957, would be the same type of large and heavy-haul freight engine as dedicated to the Cottingham morning shunt. The ubiquitous WD No.90458 was a regular example, finishing it's days at 50D Goole shed in 1967, from where it would be scrapped as steam traction finished on the North Eastern Region that year. (Noted on Marsden Rail dvd No.12 again).

The publication mentioned above, would be the very last one to contain listings of steam classes, of which just eight remained. The North Eastern Region just had one single locomotive left on its books, the K1 class 2-6-0, No.62005 which thankfully has been preserved and I saw operating *Jacobite* services in Scotland in 2002 and still does, between Fort William and Mallaig.

MEMORIES OF COTTINGHAM STATION

British Rail also possessed three narrow-gauge 2-6-2 tank engines on the Vale of Rheidol Railway in Wales until 1987 when that line was sold-off into private ownership.

When a locomotive hauled train arrived at the buffer stops, there would be some points set at the appropriate place to release the loco, but this diesel shunter needed to attach itself to the rear and pull the consist all the way out of the platform and shunt it to the sorting sidings to the north side (where St.Stephens shopping centre is today) or even as far as Botanic Gardens MPD. Classic examples of loco hauled trains would be the Brough workers extras, that Dad came home on. These would be long rakes of twelve or even thirteen suburban/non-corridor, compartment stock and I thought that the allocated class 03 diesel shunter did extremely well to haul a 350 ton-tare load out the platform all that way, albeit slowly. These high-capacity coaches were only used for short routes as no toilet facilities were available.

I will not describe the architecture of Hull Paragon Station's concourse including it's impressive restored, multi-windowed booking office entrance, as a full and detailed history can be found in Alexander Slingsby's excellent 2017 bookazine **"The Story of Hull Paragon Station, From 1848 to the Present"**.

Entering the station booking hall to access the concourse, I seem to remember seeing four booking windows on the south side but only two on the north side that were used for issuing tickets on a Saturday afternoon to supporters of *The Tigers, Hull City Football AFC* and used on the football specials to

DAVID KAY

Boothferry Park ground's single platform. I must say however, that in early 1963, the Paragon Station frontage on Ferensway had just been adorned with a modern-style, brand-new, four-storey office block labelled *Paragon House* and this had just been completed before my arrival for my trainspotting visits, as my bus passed its frontage before turning left into the bus station next door. It was used until 1970 only by BRs Divisional Headquarters staff, and most of *Paragon House* would remain dormant until it was demolished in 2006 to make way for redevelopment of the entire area. *Paragon House* was therefore the frontage to Paragon Station during this time of my frequent visits and will for ever be eched in my mind.

There was always some activity going on at Hull Paragon in the 1960s. I will leave my very favourite diesel train until later. There was sometimes a lull between 11am-12noon, when Paragon Station went deadly quiet and nothing much was happening except the odd shunting manoeuvre on either side of the platforms. The two diesel mechanical shunting engines were reduced to just one as time progressed and this was shedded at 50C, Hull Botanic Gardens diesel depot, mainly for allocated DMUs. The shunter was stabled by an office at the end of platforms 3 & 4 when not needed for work. It would have been around 1965 then, that this class 03 shunting engine was hooked up to a match truck behind the cab, in order that it was able to activate updated track circuits, due to its low weight of just 30.8tons. This was handy for the shunter to leave his pole on and therefore didn't interfere with shunting operations.

MEMORIES OF COTTINGHAM STATION

My last notable train movement at Paragon Station when my morning spotting came to a close was the arrival of the 12.8pm, DMU from Nottingham Midland via Sheffield and Doncaster. This was an extremely rare working and did not return to that Midland city. Nottingham also had a Victoria station in those days. It had left Nottingham at 8.52am and was usually formed of a pair of class 108 Derby-lightweight DMUs. It could on occasion, be a Midland Region unit with an **M** prefix to the five-digit number series. A journey of over three hours without even a buffet car and unthinkable in today's modern times! Train catering trolleys had not been invented fifty years ago. I see that it had arrived non-stop from Goole in thirty-one minutes. The Saturday working arrived five minutes later due to calling at Brough, Ferriby and Hessle. It looks like these twin units would return just to Doncaster at 12.25pm. The cleaners would board immediately and get it ready for its departure in those seventeen minutes. I would then decide my two hour sojourn on the platforms of Paragon Station were up and leave the busy terminus, hand my overdue platform ticket to the collector at the barrier and get my bus from the bus station through the side exit. I had loved every second of my morning visit to my Hull Mecca.

Just four years after first seeing Hull's most iconic and prestigious train ever, at Paragon Station's platform 8, *Yorkshire Pullman* from Hull would metamorphose into a completely different outfit called *Hull Pullman*. (Hull had had its own, Pullman-portion to London since 30th.September 1935 but this did not operate during hostilities). *Hull Pullman* would completely lose the

131

traditional Pullman livery of burnt umber and cream.

The Pullman brand had been brought over from The States by American, George Mortimer Pullman in 1873 when a fifteen year contract was initiated with the Midland Railway Company of Derby. It wouldn't be until the 1920s that the new livery would be introduced on all Pullman trains. Originally, it would have been *Midland Red* or rather crimson to start with. The contracted attendants receiving passengers and attending to their immediate needs would also disappear. *Yorkshire Pullman* would therefore overnight, lose all its elegance, glamour and pizzazz as it transitioned into *Hull Pullman* and became first class only. The same carriages would be used in the new modern version of the Pullman, but they would now become a drab medley of a reversed version of BR grey and blue with blue covering the window half of the now unnamed, former Pullman cars and grey below. The names of precious stones and ladies would also disappear. The carriages were now just referred to by their Pullman schedule numbers of E311 to E354. The older 1928 brake cars would be withdrawn. *Hull Pullman* was added to with ordinary second class passenger stock to bring the consist up to seven. The new, totally revised liveried Pullmans now carried *Pullman Class* passengers only. If the BG was still included in the train, it would now be grey for the top half and BR blue below. *Hull Pullman* I seem to remember, was put back slightly and now left Platform 8 at 1035 (note now 24-hour clock in use) on and from Monday 6th.March 1967. I have an old *Hull Daily Mail* photo taken around this time, showing this train leaving

MEMORIES OF COTTINGHAM STATION

Platform 8 at Paragon on the 'up' run to the capital with the reporting headcode 1E69. ('1' meaning express passenger, 'E' that it was bound for the Eastern Region and '69' the train number - remember that Hull was on the North Eastern Region of British Railways and coded 'N').

It is even rumoured that the once prestigious *Blue Pullman* luxury diesel unit of July 1960 and operating out of St.Pancras and Paddington stations in London, made an appearance on one or two *Hull Pullman* workings in 1973 before its final withdrawal! I actually remember very briefly seeing its yellow cab front poking out of the north end of Botanic Gardens stabling point, as it had then become, travelling to work by bus over the long since closed Botanic Gardens crossing gates. The once iconic, *Nanking blue* livery of this diesel Pullman unit had also been removed in 1967 when British Rail was being modernised. *Hull Pullman* would run for eleven years as described here until Friday 5th.May 1978. The day of the Pullman train in Britain was about over, as was the contract British Rail had had for so long with the prestigious Pullman Car Company Limited.

In order to commemorate the end of East Coast Pullman trains, a tour of the area was jointly sponsored by several railtour societies and *Travellers-Fare,* who had ended-up servicing the Pullman trains towards their demise. This took place on 20th.May 1978 and the farewell train left Kings Cross at breakfast and ran ECML to Doncaster, then Wakefield and Leeds and the Harrogate circuit round to York, where a break was taken at the NRM. The Pullman farewell special then

DAVID KAY

A Class 55 'Deltic' diesel leaves Brough for London in the 1980s 'rail blue' era. This engine would take 'The Hull Executive' all the way.

MEMORIES OF COTTINGHAM STATION

continued via Malton and Scarborough, where the locomotive,(probably a class 55 *Deltic*), would need to run round the consist as the seaside resort is a terminus. The special then proceeded onto the Bridlington line passing **Cottingham Station** and taking the Anlaby Road junction spur and continuing by way of Goole to join ECML once more at Doncaster for London, arriving during the late evening. The epoch of Pullman in Britain had come to a close, sadly forever!

Thankfully, most Pullman cars have found further uses in preservation on heritage lines, or most of the remainder are now acting as restaurants attached to public houses/inns around the UK. I believe the oldest Pullman still surviving on railway track, sits in a line of redundant vehicles in a siding at Betws-y-Coed on the Conwy Valley branch to Blaenau Ffestiniog in Wales. It is the kitchen car *Emerald* and was built in 1910 by the Birmingham Carriage and Wagon Company. It has been seen by the author on a couple of occasions. Two other Pullman cars also witnessed, are used for staff layovers and adjoin the Ravenglass & Eskdale narrow-gauge line at their headquarters on the Cumbrian coast. Even the progenitor of railway enthusiasts, Ian Allan himself had a former Pullman car as his board room; the 1921 built, twelve-wheel former kitchen first *Malaga* at his offices in Shepperton, Middlesex.

A few days later after that weekend, the timetable for a fast efficient train to London Kings Cross was once again revamped. Monday 8th.May 1978 saw the running of the first ever new train *The Hull Executive* with a completely revised departure time of around 0700hrs in order to get business travellers to the capital for mid morning. The journey time was still well over three hours calling at Brough, Goole, Doncaster and possibly one other station on the ECML. The train would now be even longer, reaching to a possible ten mark 2d air-conditioned inter-city carriages, still in blue and grey but with a mark 1 BG at one end and also a mark 1 buffet/restaurant car in the middle of the consist.

As High Speed Trains or HST125s had by now monopolised the ECML, the twenty-two Napier engined *Deltic* diesels all with names of racehorses or regiments, were now available to be allocated to *Hull Executive's* operation. I once remember seeing it leave Brough whilst on a bicycle ride. Hell, I must have been up really early! These once attractive two-tone green, 3300bhp twin engined, class 55 diesels had also been known as 'racehorses of the main line' as eight had carried short and sweet racehorse names. Thankfully D9009 *Alycidon* can still be seen today gracing our heritage and main line charter trains in BR blue with white double-arrow logo. Once again, in 1982 when the HST125 fleet had grown to its fullest potential, Hull finally became eligible to receive a set for the *Hull Executive* which still leaves Hull Paragon around 0700 but is now in London in around two-and-a-half hours, for those all important 10am meetings and conferences.

In 1986 the livery would once again be revised to the swallow, *Inter-City* colours of dark grey window surrounds with light grey lower bodywork, seperated by a wide red band. There was actually a stainless steel swallow carried on the sides of HST125 power cars (Class 43s). This would remain until British Rail was totally privatised in 1996/7 when the HST125's would

MEMORIES OF COTTINGHAM STATION

still remain on the *Hull Executive.* The operating company (TOC) would then become a series of franchised operators with names like: GNER, the state-run East Coast with its silver and pink lined mk4 coaches, Virgin Trains East Coast and today, reverts to The London and North Eastern Railway Company, but in no way connected with a company of the same name that ran a hundred years ago nearly, from 1923 to 1947. In May 2019, Hull did receive its brand new, Hitachi-Japanese built, state-of-the art Class 802 bi-mode *Azuma* breed of unit, operating with LNER and it was the first in revenue earning service for this company, spending the rest of the day on a Leeds/Kings Cross diagram. It will still be Hull's executive train but sadly not have the persona of a Pullman any longer.

The Trans Pennine, six-car DMUs were my all time favourite diesel units. Swindon works had built seventeen driving cars in 1960 and had stylish, three-screen and wrap-round corner windows at the cab ends, exactly like the Glasgow blue electric EMUs of the day. That was what appealed to me. They were inter-city stock with the feel of normal hauled coaching stock. The first, third, fourth and sixth cars were open saloon type stock, whilst the second and fifth units were motor brake seconds and of the corridor type with compartments. So the train had a total of eight B.U.T. Leyland 6-cylinder engines developing 1,840bhp. *'Trans Pennine'* trains (not to be confused with the *Trans Pennine Express* company of today) had some serious climbing to do through the Pennine hills and even through the three-mile Standedge tunnel between Marsden (NE Region) and Diggle (London Midland

Region). There was a miniature buffet car serving light refeshments and drinks over the three hour journey between Hull and Liverpool, but not full meals, hence their **RMB** (restaurant miniature buffet) status. This would be positioned third or fourth coach, depending on direction of travel. This meant that there were eight buffet cars but yet nine of the former. My calculations tell me that there were eight complete, six-car train sets with a few spare cars for repair/maintenance periods. Sets were normally shedded at Leeds Neville Hill (55H) between City station and Cross Gates and can still be seen from the main line. First Class passengers travelled in the front portion of the driving cars and the buffet car, which meant to us, looking over the driver's shoulder down the line was impracticable on these trains in second class. The driving cars, I seem to remember also vibrated alot, so therefore we tried to avoid them.

In my 1963-64 Winter NE Region timetable with its classic 'Deltic' drawing on the cover, the first departure of the morning *Trans Pennine* would be the 9.13am arriving in Liverpool Lime Street at 12.9pm and averaged three hours for the 126 mile journey. Not really impressive by today's timings, although there are no through trains these days between Hull and Liverpool, which all seems rather antiquated. I am not going to list where they called, suffice to say the main stations only, but this did include Brough. From Hull, *Trans Pennine* units ran approximately every ninety minutes throughout the day with the last one leaving at 5.53pm which took nearly four hours to cross to Liverpool arriving not until 9.39pm, but at least one could get a bite to eat! This train seemed to dawdle

MEMORIES OF COTTINGHAM STATION

between Hull and Leeds calling at most stations along the way. There were no Sunday services. One could be in Liverpool for a 10am meeting/conference by taking a local train to Leeds at 5.36am, changing there onto *Trans Pennine* from where the buffet car would be open as a few services just started and terminated at Leeds City and slotted in with the Hull workings. This would get the businessman to Lime Street station for 9.39am, again a painful four hour journey! There was also a through *Trans Pennine* train on a Sunday evening from York, arriving inbound that afternoon. The buffet car wasn't open on a Sunday.

I would witness the first arrival of the day at 11.0am during my visit to Paragon Station. They would arrive at almost two hourly intervals with the third arrival at 2.53pm coming non-stop all the way from Leeds City. Wow. That was unheard of then and this working would not even call at Selby with the then, ECML connections! It still took 58 minutes, even in those days. The last incoming service from Liverpool arrived at 6.58pm. I note that there were only five incoming services, but six going to Liverpool every weekday and Saturday. It is so so sad that not even one, class 124 unit (as the type would become under TOPS in 1973) has survived into preservation on a heritage Railway. But the memories of my favourite DMU will always be there and in lined green, not blue and grey inter-city daub with a yellow front end.

Last day on the York via Market Weighton line with a Met Camm unit at Beverley. As I say, it snowed at the end of November, 1965.

A Hull bound Birmingham RC&W Co unit at Beverley with its GT Andrews trainshed overall roof, which still exists today.

MEMORIES OF COTTINGHAM STATION

CHAPTER 10
FAMILY EXCURSIONS FROM HULL PARAGON

Sometime in June 1963, I and my brother Jonathan, Mum and and her sister, aunt Norah were waiting at the barrier gates of Platform 1 & 2 on Paragon Station. The ticket inspector kept us waiting until all the nine carriages of the hauled coaching stock had been shunted in by one of the station pilots, a diesel mechanical shunter of today's class 03 (described in Hull Paragon, my Mecca). They were maroon coaches, but not the standard mark 1 variety now becoming commonplace since their introduction in 1951. Our Withernsea train was a set of nine, LMS Stanier design stock that was thirty years old and could well have started out in the 1930s on the prestigious streamlined, art deco *Coronation Scot* running between London and Glasgow! And in a unique livery of mid blue with silver lining across the window frames to make it look even more glamorous. Even this train's locomotive was streamlined with a bullet-type nose at the front. My favourite train and steam locomotive of all times. They had class about them.

The last coach had stopped just short of the buffers. The BR man opened his gate to platform 1 to our right and we were allowed to board our stopping train to Withernsea. We were to be steam hauled, but would not have the opportunity to view the engine until disembarking at the terminus. Why was this a steam train and not the by now, ubiquitous DMU? The maximum length of a diesel unit train was usually limited to eight cars. Our train this day had nine carriages with probably more seats. Anyway, I always liked travelling compartment style, rather than in open saloon coaches. It gives one the impression you're making an important journey. Why were we having to travel in thirty-year old stock? In those days, British Railways could russle-up a complete spare train at just an hours notice. These rakes of coaches were lying about eight and nine months of the year doing nothing. They had been paid for. They were not leased and needed to earn their keep eighteen hours a day as on todays modern network. This type of old rolling stock cluttered the system from Penzance to Thurso & Wick. They could be seen everywhere in the sidings on the approach to most large and medium sized stations. Just waiting and waiting for those summer special excursion services to be arranged. We could have been travelling this day on a summer extra put on at last minute due to unprecedented demand. Today, commuters and general travellers just have to endure well-overcrowded trains and stand on many occasions due to there being no spare rolling stock, whatsoever. Plus the fact, todays trains are also shorter formations too. The fleets are kept working morning, noon and night to earn their keep for the leasing companies who own them.

    Our train filled up. It filled up even more at Botanic Gardens, at Stepney, at Wilmington and at all the remaining seven station calls on the way to Withernsea.

MEMORIES OF COTTINGHAM STATION

My Mother kept asking, 'why does this train have to stop at all the fiddly little stations?' Surely Mum could see for herself the throngs of passengers boarding along the route. The train was absolutely heaving with passengers and standing in the corridors, too. This regretfully, would be my second and very last steam train journey ever operated by British Railways. (See Steam Train to Bridlington for the first). We arrived at the buffer stops at Withernsea. The Loco was Thompson B1 class 4-6-0 No.61306 from 50B, Hull Dairycoates shed, thankfully now preserved on our heritage railways and main line certified, too. Only two of this once, 410 strong class have survived into preservation. We returned to Hull Paragon later that day by DMU train.

Thankfully in the summer months, the Withernsea branch might have just paid its way, but sadly for much of the year operated at a great loss with too many overheads, therefore it was an ideal candidate for Dr.Beeching's reshaping the railways plan and succumbed the following year, together with the sister branch to Hornsea Town....where I saw my first train way back in 1955.

One Saturday afternoon in early November 1963, Dad took his two sons to Leeds for the afternoon. Again, we left late! We caught the 1.41pm *Trans Pennine* from Paragon which took exactly an hour and we sat in the motor driving unit behind first class. It rattled and vibrated like hell. Seventeen miles out of Hull after the Brough stop, all trains heading west would pass or call at Staddlethorpe before the junction there, which turned Goole and Doncaster trains off to the left and Selby and Leeds trains would then enter the longest straight stretch of railway line in Britain to Barlby Junction, just east of Selby, a distance of thirteen miles. In 1974 Staddlethorpe was renamed Gilberdyke due to a growing, large housing estate nearby. All I remember doing in Leeds was looking for cheap restaurants in which to have a meal. If we came back on my favourite DMU of all time, it would have been the last *Trans Pennine* working of the day: 5.55pm from Leeds City, again just calling at Selby and Brough en route and taking one hour, three minutes. Obviously it was dark returning home, so trainspotting for Jonathan and I was impossible from the express diesel's carriage window, except Selby where lights shone and where we joined the East Coast Main Line for a few minutes to negotiate the notorious Selby swing bridge over the River Ouse. The tracks then negotiated Barlby Junction where the ECML went its own way north to York, now the A19 road for most of the way, running as straight as a railway track as far as Escrick.

Our parents also took Jonathan and I on many other days out in the 1960s to such places as London (1964/66/69) and in Summer 1967 we went on a 'three-day ticket' to Chester on the Monday, Morecambe on the Wednesday and Liverpool in 1964 and again on the Friday in 1967, but I won't bore readers with all this insignificant trivia. Paris for the day was the highlight of 1967 too, but regrettably not on the prestigious *Night Ferry* with sleeping accomodation. No, we had to 'slum it' on the overnight, Newhaven-Dieppe motor ferries *Villandry & Valencay* arriving at the French capital's St.Nazaire station in the early hours when commuters

MEMORIES OF COTTINGHAM STATION

were just waking from their slumbers. Needless to say, we were all total wrecks when returning to Hull after a 50 hour excursion and sightseeing, with no proper sleep!

I would like to talk about our first trip to London on 20th.August 1964. I will always remember this wonderful day out, as it was my Grandmother Kay's birthday and our first trip to the capital city. We awoke very early and excited on the alarm at 5.30am and after breakfasting, took a Richardson's London cab to Paragon Station, catching a Leeds train as far as Selby. Our York to London Kings Cross express was hauled by a *Peak* class 46 diesel No.D190 of 193 units in that class 4 power category. This is still from memory! As our train slid into Kings Cross at 11.5am, the prestigious *Master Cutler Pullman* for Sheffield Victoria via Retford, taking just short of three hours and plenty of time to serve a full luncheon menu, was waiting to leave at 11.20 in the adjacent platform, headed by the unique experimental diesel DP2. This diesel looked exactly like a *Deltic* in its smart two-tone green livery and yellow nose, but without the drone of the *Deltic's Napier* engines. Sadly, this loco got written-off in a rail disaster at Thirsk on the ECML three years later, whilst we were out on our after-school runabout ticket.

Dad wisked us around London that day in a frenzy and Mum was three-months pregnant with my sister! We mainly used the tube and even to this day, I find London Underground so facinating and exciting to travel on, although today, one must expect a massive crush of passengers most of the time. We didn't get on a single bus. Madam Tussauds, The Planetarium, The

Completed by March 1963, Hull Paragon Station's four-storey Paragon House was demolished in 2006 to make way for redevelopment and a new station frontage.

Museums. It was a flying visit to all places we called at. In 1964 London had a chain of 'fast food' outlets called *Golden Egg* and we used these in which to eat as they were quick and relatively cheap. Don't forget, Dad had four to pay for. We continued with Shackleton & Scott's Antarctic expedition ship *HMS Discovery* on Victoria Embankment used in a first, polar exploration in 1901.

I even remember coming up for 'air' from the underground, later that day on Waterloo Station (another trainspotters Mecca), to see a filthy rebuilt Bullied Pacific, West Country class engine No.34026

MEMORIES OF COTTINGHAM STATION

Yes Tor (on Dartmoor, 619m), having just arrived with an express from Bournemouth, a Weymouth Channel Islands boat train or even Devonian and Cornish resorts on the legendary and much lamented *Atlantic Coast Express (ACE)*, although by that date trains had stopped carrying their named headboard plates. So we never knew where *Yes Tor* had actually arrived from.

We continued our whip-round-London tour. Buckingham Palace, Nelson's Column in Trafalgar Square and Piccadilly Circus at night. It was August and darkness had finally fallen. We took a late breather in Hyde Park. Twelve hours on our first visit to London for all of the Kay family and it was time to make our dreary way back to Kings Cross's platform 10.

The train back home was to be the 11.55pm stopping service for Newcastle. This train was the mail and parcels too, calling at all main stations. They would be lengthy dwell times as well, as staff hurried to unload whatever was stacked in those parcel vans. This was a lengthy and heavy train, which always had a *Deltic* engine heading it, still in it's smart two-tone green and yellow nose-end. Before Peterborough, it was always Huntingdon and Hitchin and not Stevenage, which would open later in place of those two. We would disembark at Doncaster for a night time snack of cheese & tomato sandwich and a tea. The 3.17am disappeared into the night from platform 8, taking a few more hours on its journey towards Newcastle. We would change platforms. Doncaster was still alive, well and quite busy even during the small hours in 1964.

Our Brush 2-class 31 engine brought a similar empty stock train in, to load for just Goole and Hull departing at 4.5am. There would be just two passenger coaches in the consist: a brake second corridor **BSK** and a corridor composite **CK**, accomodating first class passengers, if any were about at that ungodly hour. We came to a complete standstill at Thorne Junction where the Goole and Hull line seperates from the four tracks heading for Scunthorpe, Grimsby & Cleethorpes. In 1964, there was no M18 motorway over the carriage roofs, as there would be now. We waited and waited and waited. The guard came to inform us that some timber had fallen off a goods train and it was blocking the line. Daylight was breaking. Unbeknown to us, uncle Ron, Dad's brother had gone down to Paragon Station twice already to meet us and take us home during the night, not knowing what train we were returning on. Communication was extremely poor even in the 1960s. Most of us didn't even have a telephone in our homes by that year. It was the call box on the street corner or nothing! Finally, the line was cleared after well over an hour and the train proceeded through Thorne North towards Goole. The dwell time here would be twelve minutes, as again staff spent time unloading newspapers and parcels for an early morning dispatch. Poor uncle Ron was there at Hull Paragon, standing behind the barriers to greet us in his suit and tie, even at 6.30am and to take us home. We had been away for twenty-four hours on a day trip to London and had enjoyed every single second. We were weary, exhausted and hungry but pleased with our long day excursion to London. We would do it all again two years later, but without the delay at Thorne, coming home.

MEMORIES OF COTTINGHAM STATION

CHAPTER 11
THE CLOSED DOORS OF BRITISH RAIL

As mentioned previously, I found myself at Thomas Cooks travel agency in Hull city centre in 1970. My grandparents and aunt lived next door but one to the manager of this branch, on Sutton Road. I knew that a career on the railway was sadly, going to be completely out of the question. Working on the railways, was as far as I was aware, a closed shop. This meant that they never advertised vacancies. Was a family member working on the railway? No. Did I have any friends or contacts working for British Rail? No. I only realised recently that by 1970, British Rail as it had by then been shortened to, was in serious decline. Getting in through those elusive doors was never going to happen to me as none of the above applied. Many lines, services and stations had been withdrawn and closed during my ten year tenure as a trainspotter. The blue sides of rolling stock were disgustingly filthy and never got a proper wash. Motive power was just the same and sometimes worse with spilt diesel and stains down their sides. The railways in 1970 were probably, in the most run down condition they've ever been seen in.

We would not see any improvement until 1986 when sectorised businesses would start investing in the run up to privatisation the following decade. One shining example would be the *Inter City* brand when a smart 'swallow' livery of dark grey, red and cream (actually light grey) would be introduced on the best and fastest trains. By then, my travel career was all over too and I was running a small business, working far too hard to have the time for any interest in the running of the trains or even the reading of monthly periodicals. I missed out on the railway scene for some time. But some years later when I was driving my own taxi, a customer was a driver for the then operating company *Northern Spirit*. Would me knowing him, get me a job as trainee train driver? I don't think so. By then it was 1999 and I was rapidly approaching my 47th.birthday. I was well too old to be trained up as a driver. My chances of getting through those 'railway doors' had well and truly long passed their sell by date! The chase was over but I still didn't give up. Even in recent years, I still applied to *Northern Rail* at Leeds for a post as a trainee conductor on their local services with pacer and sprinter dmus. Naturally as expected, I was in my sixties by now, but still hopeful. At least I knew I tried.

CHAPTER 12
THE MODERN SCENE

Its now June 2019 and we finally see some new trains on the Hull to Beverley, Bridlington and Scarborough line. They are refurbished, ex-Scotrail class 170 turbo diesels with three cars and look slightly sleeker! Yes, a 50% increase in seat availability. They're used on through trains, usually from Sheffield via Paragon. The class 158, 1990 'EXPRESS' units still start from Hull. The much-hated pacer units are still seen on East Yorkshire tracks and will be phased out very shortly due to not meeting persons of reduced mobility regulations, being introduced from 1st.January 2020. There is quite a step apon boarding them. The occasional sprinter & super sprinter DMU class 150 & 155/156s, also work the Hull area occasionally. And that's it. No freight, no parcels, no empty coaching stock turns and no morning shunt trip workings just to Cottingham yard.

If you are very lucky indeed, one just could witness at the weekend a couple of times a year only, a steam or diesel hauled charter, possibly from Kings Cross. This would be a long train with twelve or thirteen on (number of coaches in the consist), often with differing liveries and sometimes this is totally spoilt by having a diesel on the rear, too. This is for safety reasons in case the steam loco fails and insurance cover. Network Rail do not want a train stranded on their busy tracks. This is known as top & tailing and I just hate it. It completely spoils the appearance of the train.

And if you are really really lucky and are about on an Autumn weekday, you may even see the passing of the RHTT which only runs during the leaf fall season. The rail head treatment train will cover every line in the country where trees abound. There will probably be a Class 20 or other diesel type at the front, two blue bogie tank wagons carrying a chemical mixed with water to spray at very high pressure onto the railhead (running surface) as it passes, as leafs on the line cause a thin layer of mulch, which then makes the railhead very greasy and prone to wheelslip. There will also be an identical loco on the rear, to avoid running round at termini. I spotted this train a few years ago on an embankment in the Barnsley area as I was knocking on doors doing market research work.

My interest in the railway scene is still there and always will be. It's in my blood for life! But sadly not my trainspotting compatriots of the 1960s. I believe I may be the only one remaining, still very passionate about railways to this day. I believe they will all have other interests by now...how strange. And that is another reason for writing this book. It is a unique history of my childhood years long gone, but still very fondly remembered.

Cottingham Station is today served by its most regular train service ever. The railways of Britain are carrying more passengers than at any given time in the past, even beating record numbers between the Wars:

MEMORIES OF COTTINGHAM STATION

1918-1939 when the Big Four had just monopolised the system a few years later in 1923. Trains run up and down the Bridlington and Scarborough line at least every half hour, even well into the evening, but not quite as late as this last working on a Saturday used to do. It was the 00.01am Sundays Only (**SuO**) to Hull, last train on Saturday nights, just from Beverley. The last few trains of the evening then ran just between here and Hull. The main operating company to serve what used to be known as 'the largest village in England' is *Northern Rail*, currently owned by German operated Arriva Trains, a division of Deutsche Bahn, their state operator.

You can now catch a train at Cottingham that has started its journey in Scarborough (now hourly), or Bridlington or even just Beverley which will take you into Hull Paragon and then out again to maybe, Doncaster's new terminal platform 0, or mostly to Sheffield. About half terminate at Hull Paragon and are currently operated by class 170, three car Turbo Diesel units transferred down from Scotrail.

First Hull Trains now calls at Cottingham on its way to and from London Kings Cross calling at: (the down service), Stevenage, Grantham, Retford, Doncaster, Selby, Howden and Brough to Hull. The class 180 unit reverses here before arriving at Cottingham and Beverley, twice every weekday now and once on Sundays too. Their five-car *Adelante* units just about fills the reasonably lengthy platforms at Cottingham. Hull now has its finest and most regular service ever to the capital with seven return workings on weekdays, six on Saturdays and even five on Sundays, in addition to

A Deltic Class 55 diesel on the ECML with the Tees-Tyne Pullman in its horrible 'reversed' livery. This would be the last days of traditional Pullman trains in Britain.

The Trans Pennine in its modern guise and without buffet car, leaving York on its Sunday run to Liverpool, as described in the text.

MEMORIES OF COTTINGHAM STATION

when we were allowed out as far as the West Riding of Yorkshire and Manchester and had to be back home before nightfall. Phil and his mates even went off for several days at a time, occasionally. One mighty lucky boy just a year older than me! An interesting read, but tended to be a glorified list of engine numbers, which I felt rather spoilt it. How many would be interested?

FOOTNOTE
The demise of trainspotting.

Today sadly, you will not find a single boy or teenager standing by a railway line fence or with ABC, notebook and pen on a single railway station platform. Why? Because its becoming a hobby consigned to the history books due to standardisation. As has been mentioned a short while ago, most trains these days are of multiple unit formations and very few are locomotive hauled. There is no regular steam traffic, other than the Jacobite service in Scotland between Fort William and Mallaig. And even then, there will be only the same three engines trundling back and forth all the time with their six coach *West Coast Railways* stock.

Whenever I visit Doncaster station, yes there are trainspotters still taking down numbers! But all these are men much older than me and they're probably finding it impossible to 'kick the habit' and hoping something special comes past, like one of the brand new 'Azuma' bi-mode units on a Leeds or Hull working and now many paths on the ECML are taken by these super new trains. Ian Allan started compiling his ABC spotters companion books in 1942. I believe he was disabled and couldn't go and fight for his country in

WWII. In just over twenty years time, this generation of 'old time' spotters will have passed away and the art of trainspotting will have come into the terminus. They'll all be dead! Trainspotting may just have reached its century by 2042.

The Ian Allan brand has now been replaced by a company called Platform 5 publications of Sheffield. So your spotter's books are still available.

THE END.